ENDORSEMENTS

The "shattered spirit" is such a terrible human e:
rience and one that seems to be on the ever-grow___
increase. But the resources to address this condi-
tion or the training and tools to help those around us
seem scarce. I've referred numerous people to Mike
Hutchings knowing that he has the experience and
results so many are seeking. He is a consistent, com-
petent, and proven minister in trauma recovery. His
understanding of PTSD and his anointing to move in
healing power is unusual and welcomed in the Body
of Christ. Please allow me to highly recommend
Supernatural Freedom from the Captivity of Trauma
to you as one seeking freedom. And to those who I
know are faced with a seemingly unsurmountable
task of helping people with this terrible wound of the
soul, here is a valuable resource in leading others to
healing and freedom. God bless you as you explore
healing and freedom!

DANNY SILK
Best-selling author of *Culture of Honor*,
Loving Your Kids on Purpose, and *Unpunishable*

You may well be on the verge of reading, recom-
mending, and making use of the greatest work on the

pressing problem of trauma available anywhere. Mike Hutchings' materials (book and attendant helps) are making noticed waves of influence wherever they are used. Though having primary effect on the prevalent problems of battlefield trauma (PTSD), the work and counsel of Mike Hutchings are having great success in every area of trauma in both the old and young. As you read the book and examine the materials, prepare yourself for the astounding changes that will follow.

I have recommended Mike's works and seen significant, immediate, and continuous change on long-term as well as short-term problems with trauma. Thanks, Michael, for this significant work that is resulting in restored normalcy, saving lives, and bringing hope to thousands of people amid a generation haunted by broken thought patterns, confusion, and hopelessness.

This is the clearest, loudest, and most successful life-changing ministry in the area I know about, and I recommend it with great enthusiasm.

JACK TAYLOR
President, Dimensions Ministries
Melbourne, Florida

Living unbroken is a concept that I feel everyone would love to embrace, but for whatever reason most don't know how. Why? Because they know that maybe nothing is really wrong but something "ain't right," so to speak.

Mike, in his new book *Supernatural Freedom from the Captivity of Trauma*, helps us to understand what might be keeping us captive. The invisible captor of crisis and trauma many times grabs its victim with an invisible pain that gets hidden or overlooked because we Christians, especially those of us who have served in the military or on the front lines of ministry, get beaten up all the time and we are told just to get over it. It is one thing to tell a person who has been wounded by immature people to do that, but quite another to tell someone who has been wounded by severe trauma or crisis.

There is hope and healing from traumatic wounding. Just when you feel hopeless, grab this book and apply the contents of it to your life and watch what Father does. Mike is an excellent communicator not just in a teaching role but also in his writings. I highly recommend this book because I have seen the freedom from trauma that this book speaks of with one of my very own employees and teammates. Get it, apply it; I promise you will never feel the same again.

TRISHA FROST
Co-founder of Shiloh Place Ministries
Co-author of *From Slavery to Sonship* and *Unbound: Breaking Free of Life's Entanglements*

Mike demonstrates in this book that the answer to PTSD is the power of the name of Jesus to bring complete healing to spirit, soul, and body. Mike challenges us to do what Peter did—as he was walking, the Holy Spirit showed him a needy person (Acts 3:1-11). Peter commanded, "*Look* at us." Then he spoke healing in Jesus' name. Healing occurred, physically—the lame man stood; emotionally—he was free, so he leapt; and spiritually—he worshiped, honoring the living God who had set him free. Mike demonstrates this entire healing process from his own life's stories, teaching us the steps so we can to do the same. This *is* the church in action!

You *will* experience increased faith, passion, and power. Mike actually writes out the prayers and declarations he speaks over people, so you can pray through the healing process and experience your own healing. Then go forth to minister healing to those you meet who are hurting!

DR. MARK VIRKLER
Best-selling author of *4 Keys to Hearing God's Voice*

I meet people almost every week who have endured horrible trauma. Some military veterans experienced the horrors of war on a literal battlefield, and they now suffer from post-traumatic stress disorder, or PTSD. But many others who never served in the military were abused, overwhelmed, frightened, or victimized in other ways, and their pain is just as real as a veteran's. Everywhere I go I meet people who are suffering from a dark or difficult experience that marked them, shook them, or literally instilled fear in their hearts. This is why I am so grateful that God raised up Mike Hutchings to bring a message of freedom to victims of trauma. As long as I've known Mike, he has carried a huge burden for those who suffer from PTSD and related issues. And Mike does not just bring a clinical solution, even though he is a gifted counselor. He has discovered that the Holy Spirit can reach into our pain and break the power of trauma and fear. If you are a victim yourself or you know someone who is, this book will become an essential tool for healing.

J. Lee Grady
Author and director of The Mordecai Project

Supernatural Freedom from the Captivity of Trauma is a manifesto of hope. This much-needed work shines a bright light into an area that has remained in deep darkness for too long. We have deployed this prayer model worldwide after earthquakes, tornadoes, hurricanes, human trafficking, and theaters of war. Dr. Mike Hutchings' *trauma healing* model binds up the brokenhearted, brings liberty to the captives, and opens prison doors for the afflicted. This book is a tremendous gift to the Body of Christ.

Sean Malone
Founder, Crisis Response International

If you read only one book this year, make sure it's this one. Dr. Mike Hutchings has tackled one of the most important subjects in our world today—the healing of trauma. Through his amazing new book, *Supernatural Freedom from the Captivity of Trauma*, you will experience breakthrough for personal trauma and be equipped in a direct yet loving approach for helping others find true freedom in Jesus from the debilitation of trauma and the chaotic manifestations of its wake. I believe Dr. Hutchings' new book will become a foundational text in the years to come for both lay people and those in the mental health industry.

REVEREND JOANNE MOODY
https://www.agapefreedomfighters.org

There is no shortage of people in this world who struggle with trauma of some sort. I'm passionate about setting captives free but ministering lasting freedom to those who struggled with PTSD has always been a struggle for me as some would gain victory and others were left to continue in their struggle. Regardless, it was often a long process to wholeness. I've known Dr. Mike Hutchings for years through my connection with Global Awakening and have always appreciated his humility and compassionate heart. When I began to hear of the multitude of testimonies of those who were overcoming PTSD, I was quick to learn what

Dr. Mike was doing and emulate the process he was using. I am so glad to see this process spelled out in this book, a process that is my first "go-to" model for trauma-related ministry in both individual and large group/corporate ministry. This book gives a strong foundation before walking the reader through an activation (and if you are a minister, the activation gives you a model to use). Thank you Dr. Mike for writing such an amazing book that gives hope to the hopeless!

DR. RODNEY HOGUE
Rodney Hogue Ministries
Author of *Liberated, Getting Free and Staying Free*

Mike Hutchings thank you for this now and necessary message to the Body of Christ. As one who has been highly active in the ministry of deliverance and inner healing for 30 years, I am rejoicing that this critical key for freedom and victory is now available. Friends, our heavenly Father wants you walking and living healed and whole from all trauma and the resulting bondage of PTSD. This book is a must-read for all who have experienced and suffered trauma and have not achieved the security of the Father's love and true kingdom identity as a son or daughter. Not only will this message awaken your kingdom identity, it will impart spiritual wisdom and tools and awaken a spiritual journey of discovery that you too can walk trauma-free and emotionally and spiritually whole. You will find yourself free indeed!

REBECCA GREENWOOD
Co-founder, Christian Harvest International
Strategic Prayer Apostolic Network
Author of *Glory Warfare* and *Discerning the Spirit
Realm*

Mike Hutchings has a passion to see people set free from deep trauma and the devastation of PTSD. Many have considered PTSD impossible to cure, yet it is not impossible for God. It is God's heart to do so. Thousands of people are now free because of the teaching you'll find in Mike's new book, *Supernatural Freedom from the Captivity of Trauma*. It is filled with profound insights and testimonies of people that are enjoying the freedom that only Jesus can give. That is the gospel. Each testimony of a life being set free demonstrates the transformative love of God. Once we experience the weight of His love, freedom is the only logical result. And this book reveals the love and power of the Father available to every person. God always has a redemptive solution. We were designed to live in joy; there is no trauma deep enough to negate that truth.

BILL JOHNSON
Bethel Church, Redding, CA
Author of *Born for Significance* and *The Way of Life*

Supernatural Freedom from the Captivity of Trauma is more than a book to me. On several occasions after returning from ministering in war zones and dealing directly with the effects of terrorist attacks, I would call my friend Dr. Michael Hutchings. He ministered total freedom to me and released Jesus the Prince of Wholeness. It is a privilege to highly recommend a book with the potential to transform every aspect of your life. Free people set people free!

LEIF HETLAND
Founder of Global Mission Awareness
Author of *Giant Slayers* and *Called To Reign*

Dr. Michael Hutching's book, *Supernatural Freedom from the Captivity of Trauma*, will become an influential resource to counselors as well as a practical guide to any reader. It is a book of hope with the power of transformation. He has included stories of desperate lives that were changed through the power of truth that breaks the lies of trauma. Since all of us have suffered trauma at different levels we will receive more freedom each time we read this book. My wife, LuAnne, who had suffered abuse and trauma in her childhood that followed into her adult life, was profoundly changed by the personal ministry by Dr. Michael with the same prayers and truths that are contained in this book. Dr. Michael Hutchings is one of the foremost leaders on the subject of PTSD. Expect to be surprised by the healing love of Father God as you read, pray, and confess the truths that are contained in this book.

DALE L. MAST, Pastor
Author of *And David Perceived He Was
King, Two Sons and A Father, The Throne of
David, Shattering the Limitations of Pain*

I believe that Dr. Michael Hutching's book, *Supernatural Freedom from the Captivity of Trauma*, is a gift from the Father to our generation during a strategic time in history. Its pages are a profound experience of both personal encounter and equipping in healing prayer. Dr. Michael Hutchings courageously lifts a beacon of hope to all who suffer from trauma. He trumpets the power of Jesus to heal, extending his own story, helpful context on trauma, and remarkable testimonies that fuel faith. The content of this book is rich, vulnerable, anointed, and deeply needed. It bellows with the voice of a true spiritual father who is giving of himself for the liberty of others. Whether you are seeking healing, or seeking to be equipped as a healing minister, this book is a must read. It is pulsing with the power of Jesus to heal!

KATIE LUSE
Speaker, Author, Minister
Executive Director, ConnectUp
www.katieluse.com
www.iconnectup.net

The Lord has given Dr. Mike Hutchings something very special in the healing of trauma. Millions are plagued by a life that has been devastated by the painful things they have gone through, and despite faith in Jesus as the healer, the church has struggled to see real kingdom breakthrough for them. In this book, Mike helps us understand the effects of PTSD from a kingdom point of view, and how the Holy Spirit brings the healing power of Jesus to those suffering with the effects of trauma. Thanks to the keys the Lord has given Mike and that he shares in this book, I anticipate great breakthroughs in seeing PTSD healed and broken lives restored!

PUTTY PUTMAN
Founder, School of Kingdom Ministry

Supernatural Freedom

FROM THE

CAPTIVITY

of TRAUMA

Supernatural Freedom
FROM THE
CAPTIVITY
of TRAUMA

Overcoming the Hindrance
to Your Wholeness

MIKE HUTCHINGS

DESTINY IMAGE® PUBLISHERS, INC.

P.O. Box 310, Shippensburg, PA 17257-0310

"Promoting Inspired Lives."

This book and all other Destiny Image and Destiny Image Fiction books are available at Christian bookstores and distributors worldwide.

Cover design by Eileen Rockwell
Interior design by Terry Clifton

For more information on foreign distributors, call 717-532-3040.

Reach us on the Internet: www.destinyimage.com.

ISBN 13 TP: 978-0-7684-4627-2
ISBN 13 eBook: 978-0-7684-4628-9
ISBN 13 HC: 978-0-7684-4630-2
ISBN 13 LP: 978-0-7684-4629-6

For Worldwide Distribution, Printed in the U.S.A.

7 8 / 25 24

DEDICATION

I dedicate this book to those brave men in my family who laid down their lives to serve the United States of America in World War II so that the entire world could live in freedom today. They carried the wounds of the war in their souls for the rest of their days here on earth. They are now in heaven enjoying their reward.

My father, Clarence Hutchings, U.S. Army
My uncle, George Boone Hutchings, U.S. Army
My uncle, William Bond, U.S. Air Force
My uncle, Gordon Evans, U.S. Army,
killed in battle

I also dedicate this book to all of the amazing soldiers, sailors, and veterans who have served our country faithfully and laid down their lives so that we can be free. Your service has not been in vain, because we are still free. As of the completion of this book, an average of 22 soldiers and veterans commit suicide every day in the United States due to the wounds of the wars they carried home. This book is dedicated to ending this plague and bringing everyone home.

ACKNOWLEDGMENTS

Thank you to my amazing and loving wife, Roxanne, and to my children, Nate, Allison, and Rachel, for their patience, love, and dedicated prayers that this book might actually come into being.

A very special thank you with much gratitude to Susan Thompson for working with me for three years and refusing to give up on this work to completion. You are an incredible gift of God.

> *Father, I love You so much. Thank You for the privilege of speaking Your good news of healing and freedom and what it means to live unbroken. Your Word says to focus our minds on things above where Christ is seated at Your right hand. As we do, make us so heavenly minded that we become earthly good—that we actually give something to this world, because the world needs an encounter with You. We all need to encounter You in healing, transformation, and deliverance. Help us to understand what is available to us.*
>
> *May Your Word be the standard we continually seek to attain. May the fire*

of Your Holy Spirit come upon us and fill every place that You don't occupy already. May Your glory fill our hearts as temples of Your Holy Spirit.

In Jesus' name we pray, amen.

CONTENTS

FOREWORD

Mike Hutchings' *Supernatural Freedom from the Captivity of Trauma* is destined to become the most successful book in teaching people how to help themselves and others heal from the effects of trauma. It presents a biblical and clinical perspective on trauma, with special emphasis on the mind-body connection and the extent to which unresolved trauma effects the way we think, feel, make decisions, as well as, impacting our identity and our physical health.

Drawing upon the mission statement of Jesus of Luke 4:18 based upon Isaiah 61, Mike points to how central Jesus understood His mission was to declare good news to the afflicted, the poor, and the traumatized. This was a primary sign and wonder of the good news—the healing of the brokenhearted.

Dr. Hutchings shares insights God has revealed to him regarding how to minister to the brokenhearted, especially the traumatized. He has shared these insights in his *Healing Trauma* seminars which he has taught in thirty-two U.S. states and five other countries. Over 10,000 people have been trained and equipped in the healing prayer model presented in this book, with over 12,000 documented testimonies of those who have reported healing from all symptoms of PTSD and trauma.

I was with Dr. Hutchings when God gave him insight in how to deal with a retired army staff sergeant who was suffering physically from many issues. As we approached the sergeant, I told Mike I thought he was to lead in the ministry and I would back him up. When Mike began to minister, the Holy Spirit gave him directives regarding how to minister. The next day the sergeant was completely healed of his physical conditions which were related to severe PTSD.

A few weeks later in California another veteran came to me and shared how he needed help finding his identity that had been lost a couple of wars ago. I knew I needed Mike to come minister to this former soldier who had a diagnosis of severe PTSD from the VA hospital. Mike prayed just a few minutes with him and he too was miraculously healed. He had been told there was no hope for him and he would have to learn to manage his symptoms while on many forms of medication. This man's testimony is amazing. After this, Mike knew God had given him insight into how to minister to people who suffered from trauma, regardless of what caused the trauma. I have witnessed many traumatized people receive healing when Dr. Hutchings ministered to them.

If you want to learn how to minister to people with trauma, this is the book you want to have. I know that Mike has been asked to come to forts in the United States to minister to soldiers, as well as the front lines of the Ukraine to minister to civilians and soldiers. What psychiatrists have found daunting to bring relief, the Holy Spirit has given Dr. Hutchings the key to bring healing. I highly recommend Dr. Mike Hutchings, his ministry, and his new book.

Follow the link to hear the second soldier's story mentioned above: https://www.youtube.com/watch?v=cCwffVgvSlE.

RANDY CLARK, D.D., D.MIN., TH.D., M.DIV.,
B.S. Religious Studies

Overseer of the apostolic network of Global Awakening
President of Global Awakening Theological Seminary

INTRODUCTION

I'm a boy from Illinois. That is where I spent 58 years of my life. Both of my parents are from Kentucky. My dad and mom moved to Peoria, Illinois after World War II. My dad and three uncles were veterans of that war. A fourth uncle was actually killed in the Asian theater as a lieutenant. So we have military in our history. I'm the only Yankee on either side of the family.

I was born and raised Baptist. My folks took me to church as a child, and I went forward at age 13 to give my life to Christ. I lived like many of the

Baptists I saw around me—holy on Sundays and the rest of the week we lived a different kind of life. I eventually went off to college and majored first in theatre then in radio broadcasting. A crisis in my life caused me to drop out of college for a time. In the midst of that valley, I had an encounter with Jesus that completely changed my life, compelling me into ministry.

After about two years of ministering to youth and having a very fruitful youth ministry, God called me into pastoral ministry. The first church I pastored was in east central Illinois, in the middle of nowhere. We had about 30 people in that church. I met my wife, Roxanne, there and we became friends. I eventually returned to college and then went on to seminary, and that is when Roxanne and I started dating. We were married August 29, 1981.

I became involved in pastoral ministry in college and then seminary, pastoring part time. In 1982 we moved down to southern Illinois, to a little town called Carterville, near Marion, Illinois. About six miles away, in Spillertown, was a sister church that was part of our association of the American Baptist denomination. A fellow pastor, Randy Clark, pastored that Baptist church in Spillertown. Randy and I would meet on a regular basis as regional pastors under the authority of our regional administrator.

We got to know one another and got hungry for more of God together.

In January of 1984, Randy and I went to a James Robison Bible conference where we first met John Wimber and got connected with the Spirit-filled Southern Baptist movement. As a result of that meeting, Randy invited John Wimber to his church. John was unable to come, but he did send a team from Anaheim Vineyard led by Blaine Cook. What commenced was a series of healing meetings that completely transformed us and changed us. We encountered God's presence and all of us were baptized in the Holy Spirit. We had such an amazing encounter with God.

A majority of people from those meetings (about 150 people) were pastors and leaders from the Midwest. We used to call those meetings the "Spillertown Massacre" because we were so wrecked and ruined by God's power and presence that we couldn't go back to Christianity as we knew it. Within a year or so, most of us pastors lost our jobs. We were given the "left foot of fellowship" because, even though we didn't push it on anyone, the Spirit of God just started showing up at our churches.

How many of you reading this book know that you carry someone called Jesus within you when you accept Him as Lord and Savior? When Jesus begins to use you, He often starts showing up in ways that many people are not used to. At my church people began getting baptized in the Spirit in the middle of the night and then speaking in tongues. They would come to me and say, "Pastor, what is going on?" We all laugh at it now, but we weren't always laughing back then. It was so new to us, and we didn't know what to do with the ways in which God was showing up.

Eventually Randy left Spillertown Baptist and went to St. Louis to plant a Vineyard church. I moved back to Peoria and became part of two church plants. The changes in our lives and ministries were part of the whole adventure of moving in the kingdom of God and understanding the power and grace of the Holy Spirit. Despite challenges, life was good. I had an amazing wife and three beautiful children and eventually five grandchildren.

Over the years, I have been privileged to pastor in a Baptist context, a Vineyard context, and a non-denominational context. I also pastored a charismatic Mennonite church. That church was formed out of the charismatic movement of the 1970s. The Spirit of God moved through Mennonite churches and other congregations. I had a great staff there, and all of my kids and grandkids were around me. My wife had an incredible job as a physician's assistant.

She was happy in her career and made more money than I did. We were building a 12,000-square-foot building for a food pantry that we started. Then I went on a mission trip to Brazil with Randy Clark and everything changed.

During the trip, I was asked by Randy and the leadership of Global Awakening to come to Pennsylvania and head up Global Awakening's School of Supernatural Ministry. The offer was a privilege and I took it. But it took me two months to say yes because I wanted to know for sure that this was God. I had spent 58 years of my life in Illinois. A move to Pennsylvania would mean uprooting my life and my family and would require me to leave my church. I was happy being a pastor. Although I had received a lot of prophetic words that greater things were coming—that I was going to the nations—I found those words interesting but didn't see how they would happen. I was to learn that when God elevates you to something, it may be something that has never been on your radar.

In the midst of all of this, God provided funding for our building project in Illinois even as He began to speak to the people around me about the possibility of me leaving. I went to every circle of influence around me—including my prophetic council, the pastors I fellowshipped with, and finally my elders—seeking their wisdom and discernment. The thing I said to God was, "I have to have a yes from all these people to bless what I am doing." The elders prayed, and we wept together. Their response was, "This is what you were created for." Then they prayed for me and sent me out blessed.

When I accepted God's call as director of the Global School of Supernatural Ministry, I had no idea that He had more in mind. That "more" was to minister healing to those suffering from post-traumatic stress disorder (PTSD). That kind of ministry had never crossed my mind when we moved to Pennsylvania. Many of you reading this book have open doors in front of you. You have a decision to make about something that may involve sacrifice and hardship but also tremendous opportunity. I'm saying God is the one who opens doors. Revelation 3 tells us that God can open doors that no one can shut and shut doors no one can open. If you hear God calling you across the threshold, you may think it is for one thing, but I'm saying God has so much more for you that is not even on your radar. Trust Him.

In the 1990s, before coming to work for Global Awakening, I was involved in church planting. Whenever you church plant, most of the people you reach out to are the broken and convicted—those no one else is reaching out to. For the 12 years I was church planting, I was intentionally a vocational pastor. I worked a full-time job and also had a church. I had a master's degree in pastoral ministry and pastoral counseling and was able to turn that into a career outside of the church. I started out in adolescent and family therapy for a private practice psychologist and ended up in social work, working as a clinical coordinator for homeless youth and runaways. I supervised 13 counselors who went out on the streets to serve homeless youth. If they were underage and ended up in a police station, we helped them. I also worked in the foster care system. In the course of all of this I encountered a lot of trauma—people acting out based on trauma.

There was about a year or so when I started counseling people who were survivors of satanic ritual abuse. I knew about the subject but had not pursued research on the subject. Back in the 1990s, there was very little written about this subject. I learned of a psychiatrist, James Friesian, who wrote the book *Uncovering the Mystery of MPD,*[1] which is now known as dissociative identity disorder. I learned some things from studying his work, but that was my only exposure to satanic ritual abuse. At that time nothing was offered by the church; treatment for these people was only done in a secular context.

My first opportunity to minister healing for trauma came through Global Awakening. I was with Randy Clark at a healing school in Urbana, Illinois in November of 2012. A man came to me and asked if Randy could pray for him for PTSD. "I'm a veteran," he said. "I have chronic nerve pain. I can't sleep at night. I have night sweats, nightmares, and night terrors. Would you ask Randy to pray for me?"

"I'll ask him," was my response.

When I asked Randy, his response was for me to pray for the man. "I'll stand with you, but you pray for him," he said.

As I stood there ready to pray, the first thing I did was to ask Holy Spirit what He wanted me to do, and right away I got direction. I got a download from the Lord about the specific steps to take with this man. One of them was to have him look in my eyes. It's hard to look anyone in the eyes for any length of time, especially when it's man to man. Men just don't gaze into each other's eyes. Yet this is what the Lord wanted me to do. At some point as I was praying for this man, he became overwhelmed with the Spirit and dropped to his knees. Then he began to shake and his eyes rolled back into his head. After a couple minutes, he got up and said, "I feel free. All my pain is gone." He came the next morning to the conference and told me, "I had the best night's sleep I've had in five years. I had no night sweats, terrors, or nightmares. All my fear and anxiety are gone."

After his healing, he began to pray for veterans in his church, and they too were healed. His wife, who had suffered from severe health issues, was healed and her scheduled surgery cancelled. God lunched the two of them into a ministry to veterans and active-duty soldiers, many of whom have been set free from the trauma that comes from being in war.

When Randy asked me to pray for this man, I didn't know how to pray for someone with PTSD. I had been praying for people for physical healing for 30 years but never for someone with PTSD. Not knowing what else to do, I simply followed John Wimber's five-step prayer model. According to this prayer model, when someone presents for physical healing, the first thing you do is pray silently, "Holy Spirit, what do *You* want to do here?" That is what I did that first night, and here I am years later and I've had the privilege of training close to 10,000 people in the U.S. and in five other countries around the world to pray for healing from PTSD. We have verified testimonies of over 12,000 people who have been healed of the symptomology of trauma and PTSD.

There will be times when someone in spiritual authority in your life will ask you to do something that you aren't comfortable with because you have never done it before. You will feel disqualified. Yet when you are willing to step into the assignment, you will find that it comes with an anointing to carry out that assignment. It's been said that God doesn't necessarily call the equipped; He equips the called. This has been true for me and I have seen it happen with many others. Don't let lack of experience keep you from what God has for you. He's not worried about your lack of experience, so you shouldn't be either.

Post-traumatic stress disorder is not confined to those in the military. Anyone who has experienced trauma can suffer its effects. The finished work of the cross gives humankind access to God's covenant blessing of wholeness and completeness. God wants to heal our physical bodies and get us spiritually healed as well. He desires to heal every aspect of who we are. The Father's heart for all of us is beautifully expressed in Third John 2: *"I pray that you may prosper in all things and be in health, just as your soul prospers"* (NKJV). I have seen thousands healed from trauma. You too can experience God's healing and walk in wholeness. Jesus has made a way and He is inviting you to walk in it.

NOTE

1. James G. Friesen, *Uncovering the Mystery of MPD* (Portland, OR: Wipf and Stock, 1997).

CHAPTER 1

LIVING UNBROKEN

W hat does it mean to live unbroken? To begin with, we need to understand our identity—who God created us to be. Each one of us is made in the image of God, but most of us are not living with a sense of our true identity because we haven't been taught about identity. What we have been taught is to look to the world or to ourselves for an understanding of who we are. When you are living without a sense of your God-given identity, you are going to live a life far removed from the plans God has for you. This is illustrated in Acts 3:1-11. In these passages Luke is telling us about a miracle that took place immediately after Pentecost—the healing of a man who had been lame for 40 years, from the time he came out of his mother's womb.

> *Now Peter and John went up together to the temple at the hour of prayer, the ninth hour. And a certain man lame from his mother's womb was carried, whom they laid daily at the gate of the temple which is called Beautiful, to ask alms from those who entered the temple; who, seeing Peter and John about to go into the temple, asked for alms. And fixing his eyes on him, with John, Peter said, "Look at us." So he gave them his attention, expecting to receive something from them. Then Peter said, "Silver and gold I do not have, but what I do have I give you: In the name of Jesus Christ of Nazareth, rise up and walk." And he took him by the right hand and lifted him up, and immediately his feet and ankle bones received strength. So he, leaping up, stood and walked and entered the temple with them—walking, leaping, and praising God. And all the people saw him walking and praising God. Then they knew that it was he who sat begging alms at the*

*Beautiful Gate of the temple; and they were
filled with wonder and amazement at what
had happened to him. Now as the lame
man who was healed held on to Peter and
John, all the people ran together to them in
the porch which is called Solomon's, greatly
amazed* (Acts 3:1-11 NKJV).

There is a word in the Old Testament that many
use as a greeting, which is the word *shalom*. *Shalom*
means peace, but it also has a deeper, richer meaning.
Shalom is a covenant blessing that refers to wholeness,
completeness—a sense of living in a place where you
lack nothing because of what God has given to you in
His covenant. God desires that we all live in the fullness of His *shalom*.

You will recall that prior to the healing of this
lame man, Peter and John had experienced a baptism of fire from the Holy Spirit in Acts 2. Scripture
tells us that they were counted among the 120 who
were meeting in an upper room where they had been
for ten days, praying after Jesus appeared to them
before ascending to heaven. As they were praying
on the day of Pentecost, the Spirit of God fell upon
them as tongues of fire on their heads, causing them
to speak in other tongues. The noise from the Spirit
of God that accompanied this baptism of fire was so

loud it drew scores of people to the building where the upper room was located.

As God would have it, there were thousands in Jerusalem for Pentecost representing all the nations of the world to which the Jewish people had been scattered. As they came together at the sound of the noise of the Holy Spirit, they were positioned by God to hear Peter give one of the greatest sermons in the Bible. In answer to their questions about what was going on, Peter told them, "this is that" which was spoken of in the Old Testament through prophets—that the Spirit of God would descend and fill the hearts of all the people. What happened on Pentecost that day was an amazing harvest of souls with 3,000 coming into the kingdom.

Fast-forward a few weeks or perhaps a few months from Pentecost and we find Peter and John going to the temple daily to worship God, where they encounter the lame man and, through them, God heals the man. It is important to understand something about Peter and John. They were not perfect and they didn't necessarily have experience for the things God was going to ask them to do. Just a short time before Pentecost they were part of a disheveled band of disciples who had fallen asleep in the garden of Gethsemane when Jesus asked them to pray. They denied Jesus on the night of His

arrest and abandoned Him before the cross, fleeing instead. Only John went to the cross. Their bold
declarations of loyalty quickly gave way to betrayal
and abandonment. It was only a short time between
their moments of failure and the time when the
Spirit of God came upon them as fire that they were
used mightily to bring 3,000 to salvation and heal a
man who had been lame for 40 years.

No matter how much you feel like you have
failed, the good news is that you are not disqualified thanks to the power of the grace of God. Even
though you have not seen the kind of miracles and
transformation you've cried out for, that does not
mean you are disqualified. Much of the lack of healings and miracles in ministry simply has to do with
believing the lie of the enemy that says because
what you've done is so bad, the blood of Jesus is
not sufficient to cleanse you and bring you back to
a place of restoration. No one who declares Jesus
Christ their Lord and Savior is disqualified from
doing the very same things Peter and John did in
Acts, which was to bring restoration and healing to
a broken person. One could easily say that because
of their severe failings, Peter and John should have
been sidelined from ministry for a time, or for good.
But Jesus had another plan. Scripture says *as they
were going*—how interesting is it that as you read

the gospels and the book of Acts, some of the most significant healing miracles take place *as people are going* from one place to the next? They were not standing in a church declaring the gospel. Yes, there were miracles in the synagogue, but a greater number of miracles took place as the disciples *went*. This tells me that God is as interested in bringing miracles in all the journeys we take on a daily basis as He is in bringing the miraculous to bear within the four walls of the church.

GOD'S SHALOM

The healing of the lame man in Acts 3 represents what I believe shalom really means, which is God's covenant blessing of wholeness and completeness. There is another New Testament term, *sozo,* that often refers to salvation and also means "deliverance." To experience *sozo* is to be healed, delivered, and set free—to experience God's shalom. Here we have a man who has led a traumatic life from the moment he was born. He has what we refer to today as a birth defect. He is totally lame with no ability to stand on his own. In the Jewish culture of his day, if you were disabled you were considered cursed. So from the moment he came out of his mother's womb, he was not only disabled, he was cursed. The belief at that time was that birth defects were the result of sin of the parents. So not only was he cursed, but his parents had a cloak of shame put upon them as well. The only thing this lame man was valuable for in that culture was to sit on the street every day and beg for alms.

Now, this man was obviously smart because he positioned himself at the entrance to the temple. Jews were required to go to the temple to worship God on a daily basis, and so it follows that there was a lot of foot traffic at the entrance to the temple. In addition, there was a provision in Jewish law that if you gave alms to a poor person it was considered an act of worship. Any Jew about to enter the temple could simply give the lame man some money and then be on his way, having performed his act of worship for the day.

Jewish law also said that if you had a defect in your body you weren't allowed in the temple to worship God. For 40 years this man couldn't go in the temple. He was cut off from the spiritual life of his culture. What's interesting is that if this man had been sitting daily at the temple entrance for 40 years, then Peter and John must surely have walked by him before. It would follow that the other disciples had walked by him too, as well as Jesus. This speaks to me about the timing of God.

Many contend for healing for others and yet many times we don't see it and wonder why. Many of us are dealing with situations in our own bodies, struggling in need of healing that has not yet come. Why? I'm not saying God holds out for the perfect time. What I am saying is that time is in God's hands. We are called to obey Him in that moment when He puts someone in front of us and tells us to act.

If I had said no when Randy asked me to pray for the man with PTSD, I would have missed an opportunity to step into something with God that has certainly been an amazing privilege to see. In that moment when Peter and John walked by the lame man, whom they had likely walked by before, I believe by the power of the Spirit they "saw" him and were prompted to act. Scripture says that Peter instructed the man to "look at us." Beggars were not allowed to look at the people who were coming into the temple. The man's head would have been bowed, his eyes downcast. When Peter invited him to look up, he lifted up his head in a moment of faith, expecting to receive money from Peter. Here was a man who had more faith to receive than many who sit in the pews every Sunday in our churches today. He was what we call an unbelieving believer as opposed to a believing unbeliever. So often it is easier to bring healing to those who have not been in church because they have no religious strongholds that have taught them not to expect much from God. They are desperate and will take anything. That is why it is easier to pray for people outside the church than in the church.

What happened next is one of my favorite parts of the story. Peter made a declaration that changed the atmosphere. He told the man that he didn't have money for him; he had something better. Peter believed that the power of the name of Jesus was as tangible, as strong as any bit of money he could give the man. What the man needed was not silver and gold but the power of the name of Jesus to bring healing and restoration to his life.

Here is my question for you: Do you understand how powerful it is every time you speak the name of Jesus into the atmosphere? I know it is powerful because the enemy never uses the name Mohammed as a curse word. He never uses the name Buddha as a curse word. People curse with the name of Jesus because there is power in the name. When believers use the name of Jesus powered by the Spirit of God, we are releasing that power to every situation we find ourselves in.

The lame man has his hand out to receive what he thinks will be money as he lifts his eyes to Peter.

Instead, as Peter grabs his hand the man rises up with a leap and stands on his own two feet for the very first time in his entire life. Then he begins to walk, leap, and praise God. If you have ever been sick for a while in bed, you know it takes a few weeks to have the strength to walk again. Imagine if you have never walked in your entire life like this man. What he experienced was a creative miracle where his muscles, tendons, and joints all came into perfection again so that not only did he jump up— he was able to walk, leap, and praise God. Those three actions are symbols of the *shalom* of God, of what it means to live unbroken. Walking meant he was physically healed. Leaping and praising God meant he was emotionally healed. There was joy in his heart because he understood that the healing he received was not from Peter and John but from God.

Something else happened in that moment of healing as he was walking, leaping, and praising God; he went with Peter and John into the temple. For the first time in his life, he went into the temple to worship and pray to God. His entire life—physical, spiritual, and emotional—had been restored by a miracle in Jesus' name. Why is this important to you and me? It is important because as believers who are called to minister healing, we need to understand that God is after all of us. He doesn't just want to heal our physical bodies. He's not just interested in getting us spiritually healed. He wants to heal every aspect of who we are. In Third John 2, John writes to his children, *"I pray that you may prosper in all things and be in health, just as your soul prospers."* This is God's heart for all of us.

God is very serendipitous. Just about the time we think we know the plans He has for our life, He comes along and gives us something more. I never could have imagined that I would be used by God to minister healing to those who are suffering from PTSD all over the world. Yet it is a great privilege to be used by God in this way. He knew how my heart was already drawn in this direction from having witnessed the suffering of members of my own family. My dad and four of my uncles were in World War II. They returned home different—traumatized. There is a stigma upon soldiers and veterans regarding post-traumatic stress disorder. They are sometimes accused of "having" this disorder just to get disability benefits. That is a lie.

I once sat with a congressman and talked about this issue of PTSD in the military. He said his dad came back from World War II, and they never talked about it and everything was okay. He thought too much attention was being put on post-traumatic stress disorder. I responded, "What I see is that men and women are severely tormented. They just want to get well. They don't want to carry the label of PTSD because it is a symbol of weakness. The trauma they've experienced is impacting their lives in such a way they can't work a regular job." I then told him the story of my uncle.

George Boone Hutchings, my father's older brother, joined the army right after Pearl Harbor. He was part of the first wave of troops sent over-seas into North Africa. The Allies took quite a large amount of shelling, and my uncle was injured. He was sent home to a military hospital in New Jersey, and then transferred to the psychiatric ward because of shell shock. He spent three years there and could not return to active duty. He was not medically discharged nor honorably discharged, but just dis-charged. It was apparent in the years after the war that the federal government sought to deny and downplay the effects of the war trauma on men's souls. If a soldier or veteran shared problems they were experiencing, it was considered a weakness. If you've seen the movie *Patton*, you likely remember the scene where he goes in and slaps the young sol-dier who is battle fatigued and calls him a coward.

My uncle came out of the military, married his high school sweetheart, and within a year they were divorced. He spent the rest of his life in loneliness as an alcoholic. He moved to Peoria where my family lived and became like a second father to me. He was amazing and generous, but something would happen and he'd flip a switch and become angry and raging. We'd hear that he would start fights. He would isolate himself for weeks on end. I remember one time, as a nine-year-old boy, going to his trailer with my dad to check on my uncle because he had emphysema. My dad knocked on the door, and I remember to this day hearing my uncle scream at the top of his lungs from the back of his trailer—cursing and saying to get out. He said he was done with us. He knew who we were. He threated to kill us. I remember crying. My dad said my uncle's behavior was because of the war.

My uncle died as a Christian, but now I know what he suffered. Studies have shown a strong link between addictions and trauma.[1] We in the inner healing movement have known this for years—that just about all addiction is related to some kind of trauma in a person's life that they are trying to deal with. It is good to see that there are now scientific studies that have made that link. I have a friend who heads up a treatment center, and through our association I hear that the entire addiction industry is shifting their way of dealing with addiction from behavior-focused to trauma-focused. They are realizing that most addictive behavior has some kind of trauma attached to it. We still have so much to learn. I am learning every day and I thank God for being my teacher. He and all the dear men and women I have had the privilege of ministering to have taught me so much about what life looks like when the God of all love touches and heals a life marred by trauma.

In the chapters that follow, we will examine trauma as a soul injury, looking at its effect on the mind and body, as well the schemes of satan to torment the traumatized. Through testimonies of freedom, we will see how healing prayer closes access to the spirit of trauma, bringing revelation of God's heart to restore and heal the whole person.

NOTE

1. Lamya Khoury, Yilang L. Tang, Bekh Bradley, Joe F. Cubells, Kerry J. Ressler, "Substance use, childhood traumatic experience, and Posttraumatic Stress Disorder in an urban civilian population," *Depression & Anxiety* 27(12), 2010, 1077-1086, accessed June 9, 2020, https://www.ncbi .nlm.nih.gov/pmc/articles/ PMC3051362.

CHAPTER 2

UNDERSTANDING TRAUMA AS A SOUL INJURY

Most everyone who lives long enough will experience some kind of trauma. In this chapter, we are going to look at the signs and symptoms of PTSD. Having one or two of the symptoms doesn't mean you have PTSD. Post-traumatic stress disorder is when a combination of symptoms impacts your life in a negative way causing you to develop an anxiety disorder that prevents you from living a healthy and productive life. Let's begin by reviewing a clinical definition of post-traumatic stress disorder.

> PTSD is a common reaction to trau-
> matic events. Many people recover in
> the ensuing months, but in a significant
> subgroup the symptoms persist, often
> for years...PTSD becomes persistent
> when individuals process the trauma
> in a way that leads to a sense of serious,
> current threat.[1]

Traumatic events may trigger PTSD and include violent personal assaults, natural or unnatural disasters, accidents, or military combat. Anyone who has gone through a life-threatening event can develop PTSD, including military troops in war; rescue workers such as those who responded to 9/11; survivors of accidents, rape, sexual abuse, or other crimes; immigrants fleeing violence in their countries; survivors of hurricanes, floods, or earthquakes; and those who witnessed such events. Family members can also develop PTSD. This can be a crippling disorder affecting the ability of the sufferer to live everyday life.

SIGNS AND SYMPTOMS OF PTSD

Flashbacks

PTSD sufferers can become upset when reminded of traumatic experiences or actions in the course of day-to-day life causing their mind to flash back to that traumatic experience. You experience things with your five senses, and something triggers a flashback that takes you right back to that place. It takes you out of the reality you are in and into that prior experience. For instance, a smell may come to you and trigger a flashback to a traumatic experience associated with that smell. You may see something on TV or outside, maybe in a crowd, that causes you to remember something. Veterans may hear something such as fireworks that take them back to the battlefield. The highest incidence of suicide among veterans with PTSD occurs on the July 4th holiday.

When flashbacks happen there is this feeling of being out of control of your life. You are never sure of what is going to happen. This can create a tremendous amount of insecurity. A lot of folks with PTSD will isolate themselves and may not go outside much. They become agoraphobic and stay in one safe place, never venturing out.

A 74-year-old woman came to me for prayer ministry. She had suffered much physical and sexual abuse at the hands of her parents as a child. Leaving home as a teen to escape the abuse, she took a night job and was brutally raped on her way home from work one night. She suppressed much of this for many years, throwing herself into work as a way to escape. When she began to work with abused and battered women, flashbacks haunted her. Her health declined. She was diagnosed with multiple sclerosis and functional neurological disorder. Eventually she needed an electric scooter to get around. A friend suggested Christian healing and invited her to a conference where she received ministry for PTSD. She told me:

> This gave such a breakthrough in my spirit and in my mind. I felt safe in God's hands. It was like clean new windows to see the truth and face the truth. I could wholeheartedly say it was the Holy Spirit's work...God gets the glory every time. He walked this journey closely with me, providing the right people at the right time to heal me from PTSD, which had formed a physical stronghold in my mind and body. This released damaging memories from my mind... God spoke the word "forgiveness" to me knowing I was ready to deal with this and come to a place knowing I needed to forgive the abusers. After eight months and no medication, I have been pronounced non-clinical for PTSD, no MS and no functional neurological disorder.

God's work has made new pathways in my brain...my body is strengthened, I no longer need a walker, electric scooter, or my walking stick most of the time. I have even climbed back on my bicycle for a short ride. Freedom from rejection is another mountain conquered. I hope this story encouraged you to take the next step with God wherever that might take you. He cares for you.

Nightmares

PTSD sufferers have nightmares or vivid memories. These occur during waking hours and when they sleep. For veterans and first responders, they may have a nightmare about something they've experienced either on the battlefield or in service. Obviously, civilians can have these types of nightmares as well. What happens many times with veterans is that they have such vivid nightmares that they wake up thrashing and trying to break out or beat the person in their nightmare. Many times, they may actually attack their spouse. There are a number of men I've prayed with who have had a spouse wake up with hands around their throat. At its worst this kind of behavior causes divorce. Those experiencing night terrors can also have night sweats, where they drench the bed in sweat.

I was in South Africa with a pastor who is planting churches in the Zulu nations, in Zimbabwe and Zambia. He was traumatized by his time in the military in South Africa. He would wake up in the middle of the night and stand up and try to run. Many times, he would run out of the tent and find himself in the middle of the jungle in the middle of the night, not knowing where he was. His wife would talk about how he would wake up and stand up straight in bed or attack her. I prayed for him and God completely healed him.

Emotional Numbness

A third sign of PTSD is a sense of being numb or losing interest in things you used to care about. When this happens, people feel disconnected from themselves. Things they used to love or enjoy they now have no feeling toward whatsoever. They may not have feelings about anything. If any emotion is felt, it is rage and anger. They get into a zombie-like state where they can't feel excited, happy, or sad about anything in life. It is like being outside of yourself, and you cannot connect to your life or other people. You feel numb all the time, which is a perfect place for the spirit of suicide to come.

Depression, Anxiety, Irritability

Depression, anxiety, jitteriness, and irritability are also symptoms of PTSD. There is a sense of irritability that comes upon the person causing those around them to have to "walk on eggshells." The least little thing can set off people in this state of mind. They may start throwing things or physically abusing others. Afterward, the person is remorseful because the flash point of the rage comes from a place they can't even identify. Depression sets in because life has become hell.

Hypervigilance

Another sign of PTSD is being overly alert and aware of potential threats. For military and first responders, this is a part of their mental training. Battlefield training doesn't leave you. When you come out of the military, they don't give an on/off switch. The mental training that served you well on the battlefield does not serve you well as a civilian. It makes you paranoid. You're always expecting things to happen. Wherever you are, you can walk into a room and scan the room and sees threats. You never sit with your back toward the door. It is difficult to be in crowds because you don't know who presents a threat. You live with a sense of hypervigilance. Wherever you are, if it is not your safe place, you are on alert for threats. This sets up stress, paranoia, and a sense that no place is safe.

Chronic Nerve Pain

PTSD sufferers may experience chronic nerve pain, which is an undefined pain in their bodies. This can also be called fibromyalgia, which is a sense that the nervous system is inflamed. A VA doctor explained that this happens when the effects of traumatic experiences set up a hormonal imbalance within the adrenals and endocrine system, which includes glands like the thyroid, causing them to pump out hormones on a regular basis. Military training teaches you how to keep your adrenals flowing. When these glands are triggered, they trigger the amygdala in your brain, which is responsible for the fight-or-flight hormones. Imagine adrenaline flowing all the time triggering your flight-or-fight response. Over time this significantly impacts your nervous system causing inflammation and chronic nerve pain. When ministering to someone who suffers with fibromyalgia, I ask how long they've had it, then I ask if something happened before the onset of the chronic nerve pain. Nine times out of ten, you'll find someone who had a traumatic event prior to the onset of chronic nerve pain.

Insomnia

Difficulty sleeping or insomnia is another sign of PTSD. Those suffering trauma can only sleep little bits at a time. Many get less than three hours of sleep per night. My wife, who has a background in sleep medicine, told me the worst torture you can impose on someone is sleep deprivation—it can make a person go crazy. Imagine these folks for whom sleep is not safe. They can't sleep and often wander around at night. There is a sense of torment. If you can't escape the trauma of the day with a good night's sleep, you are even more tormented.

Inability to Focus

Another sign of PTSD is having trouble keeping your mind focused on one thing. I have prayed for men and women who have performed excellently on the battlefield, but when they come off their entire mindset changes. They are confused and depressed. They are unfocused and can't keep things straight. Their bills go unpaid, their house is a mess. Everything is in a chaotic state, and it is because of trauma. Here is one man's story of healing:

> I am an army veteran who was injured in battle and suffered PTSD for years. I struggled with depression, anxiety, and

chronic pain. I couldn't sleep at night. All of this caused me to slip into depression and isolate myself from others. At times I couldn't concentrate or think straight. While working on an advanced degree, I had a breakdown and had to drop out of school and quit my job. I was lost. I almost lost my family. My wife was the rock who supported me and kept us afloat.

When Mike prayed for me, he prayed healing over my mind, body, and spirit. Then he had me hold my hand over my heart as he prayed for my spirit while I confessed myself to Jesus once again, recommitting my life to the Lord. Next, he asked me to put my hands on my head as he prayed for my mind and specific parts of my brain. He also prayed for my body to be healed of pain from multiple injuries.

From the moment Mike prayed for me, I experienced a change like no other. My mind became clear and I am able to sleep now. I don't need to take nighttime meds because the nightmares are gone. Mentally I feel like a new person. I still have a little pain in my body but nothing like before. I now know that God does love me and that He didn't ever leave me. He sure came to save me that day Mike prayed for me.

Addictions

PTSD sufferers will often use alcohol, drugs, or pornography to numb feelings. Most folks who are trying to deal with trauma use alcohol and legal or illegal drugs. Many men also use pornography to deal with trauma. I have learned of another drug of choice because I've had the opportunity to pray for successful businessmen. Some deal with their trauma through success and become workaholics. They work 80 hours per week by strength of will. The reality is that many are severely traumatized, and they find relief by working non-stop.

Over-Medication

One of the things you have to understand, particularly about veterans, is that the VA does not consider PTSD to be curable. They use medication and coping mechanisms and counseling. When PTSD sufferers are treated in this way, they begin to tolerate the medicine to such an extent that they have to keep changing meds. They begin to feel like zombies. I know of one testimony where the man was taking 60 pills a day. He had pills to deal with side effects from other pills. I am not against medication, but this kind of thing—allowing prescription drugs to overtake people until they become their drug of choice—is not the answer.

Suicide

PTSD sufferers may consider harming themselves or others. A demonic spirit of suicide is part of this disorder. This demonic spirit says, "Life is hell, you're no good, just kill yourself." Right now in this country today, 22 veterans or active duty soldiers are committing suicide every day. We have lost more veterans and soldiers to suicide than we did on the battlefield in Iraq and Afghanistan. This is because of PTSD. When I hear of a shooting around a military base, I can pretty much guarantee that is a person who has lost hope because of their trauma. They are raging at that point, and the only thing they know to do is go hurt the people who say they can help but don't help.

There is also what is known as "suicide by cop." This is where you have a veteran who has lost hope. They want to commit suicide, but they know if they do their family will not get benefits. They point a gun at someone, police are called, then they point the gun at the police and the police shoot them.

There are a few active duty military bases where this is occurring in epidemic proportions.

Isolation

PTSD sufferers often pull away from other people and become isolated in an effort to cope with what is going on within them. This kind of isolation often ends tragically. The worst wounds may be the ones you cannot see. Many are suffering from traumatic brain injury (TBI). Among suicide cases, 18 to 20 percent have experienced a TBI (traumatic brain injury), which is also part of PTSD. This is all very depressing, but there is hope and healing in Jesus' name. Here is a testimony of hope and healing.

> I had a lifetime of abuse—abuse from my father and abuse from my spouse as well. I have experienced very traumatic things since I was a child. I've had night terrors my whole life, which is 50-plus years. I've not been able to sleep a whole night through in over forty years. Exhaustion was a regular part of my life. Night terrors continued after my spouse died. My spouse chose to commit suicide, which was equally traumatic.
>
> I went through the training for healing PTSD, and I realized that something was

still bothering me even after intensive therapy for several years. I just couldn't break free and couldn't sleep. What I figured out was that a portion of this PTSD healing cuts off soul ties. After we walked through all of those pieces and basically cut the soul ties that were still attached to me from my spouse and father, that night I slept the whole night for the first time. It was sweet bliss. My short-term memory came back the next morning, which was really a surprise and added bonus. I don't feel like I'm going crazy anymore. I don't feel tired when I get out of bed. What I realized was that I finally have freedom. This is just utterly miraculous. I just stand in utter awe. What I walked through in a couple of minutes did more for me than years of therapy.

Even though the Lord had filled my heart, and I had a lot of faith and hope and managed things, I wasn't free or healed. Don't live with it. There is a really wonderful option, and it is just going through this training and trusting the Lord. You can have this freedom. Take it, and I wish you the best.

ADDRESS MENTAL TRAUMA IN THE CHURCH

One of the greatest issues in the church today in America is the issue of mental health. As much as we are seeing an amazing rise in physical healings and salvations, the question remains, "What is the church doing about mental trauma?" For many of us in charismatic and Pentecostal streams, we tend to put mental trauma and mental illness in the category of deliverance, telling people that if they have a mental disorder they have a demon. This is a lie that shames people and makes them feel hopeless. It makes them feel unworthy.

It seems that we in the church have decided we don't want to have to deal with mental health issues because we don't know what to do them. Perhaps we don't know what to do because we have not asked God for the key to bringing healing to people's souls—how they think, how they feel, how they choose, and their identity. We would rather tell people to read the Bible more, pray more, and come to church more, and just "get over it." For years that is what some in the church have been telling folks who carry trauma. Let me be clear—you don't *get over* trauma.

What happens instead is that people become ashamed because they are not living the kind of life that we project from the platform where everything is good, perfect, and whole. The reality is that God is bringing mental health issues to our doorstep because He has the answer for all mental illness. He has the answer for the rise in suicide that is taking place not only in the military community but also in the first responder and millennial community and in all of society. The enemy seeks to kill and destroy the plans God has for each person's life. The good news is that God is giving the church the keys to bring healing to trauma of the mind. Our first response is to acknowledge and receive these keys.

In the same way that Peter and John could say to the man, "rise up and walk," so we have the power and authority to bring healing, restoration, and complete recovery to those who are walking in mental trauma, but it means we have got to walk with them. Gone are the days when we would go down the prayer line and say, "be healed, be healed, be healed," and people would fall over and that was it in terms of ministering to them. There is a supernatural power that brings healing to people, but after that healing we have got to walk with some of those people. There has to be a healing community within our churches that walks with people through the process of being restored in Jesus' name. Walking with someone through the healing process is not a quick fix. Restoration can take time. Some experience instant restoration, but for most it is a process.

There is power in the name of Jesus and in community as we bring people in and walk with them through this process of healing in Jesus' name. Bipolar disorder is not a hopeless disorder one can never be healed of. Schizophrenia is not something one can never be healed of. Alzheimer's, dementia—these are not hopeless disorders. Depression, anxiety, and panic attacks are not hopeless. The reality is that we have become so focused on getting information into people's minds that we ignore what needs to happen in their hearts. In the 1950s there were movies about aliens with giant heads and tiny hearts. That is a picture of what we are doing to people in the church. We are filling their heads with so much information about healing while neglecting to lead them to a revelation of God's love that must fill our hearts so that complete healing can take place. No matter how much information you pour into someone, unless they have the revelation of God's love in their heart, they won't have a transformation. And unless they experience that transformation in community, there will likely not be complete healing because it is very hard to walk out this kind of transformation alone.

We are to live as authentic people created by God to be joyful, but He has also given us the capacity to feel sadness, anger, and loss. We are not to be a Vulcan, Spock-like people where bad and negative emotions are forbidden and everyone is happy, happy, happy. Let's create a safe place for authenticity. Sometimes we just need Jesus with skin on to pray for us. When someone asks how you are, instead of saying "fine" when you're not fine, it should be okay to say, "I'm struggling today. Would you pray for me? I'm struggling today. I need help. Can you bring the love of God to me?" I believe the greatest expression of *shalom*—of wholeness—is when we can be our authentic selves. The authentic self is not a perfect person who never has a bad day. The healthiest hearts are not found in those who have no problems, but those who have found their heart's true home in God. What that means for you and for me is that we come to understand that Jesus cares as much about our soul and the health of our soul as He does about our spirit and our body.

We live in the greatest days of opportunity—opportunity to see the greatest harvest of souls the world has known. Most of the folks who are being gathered in are not coming from within our churches; they are coming from the streets. A number of years ago our government gave up the responsibility of caring for the mentally ill, cut funding for places where the mentally ill could go to be cared for, and basically put them on the street. That is our homeless population today—the mentally ill, veterans with PTSD, and people who deal with addiction. I believe God is looking at this sad situation and saying, "Where is My church?"

When you really become purposeful about bringing the power of Jesus into a community, you will experience persecution that can bring with it trauma. The question then becomes, "What are you going to do with that trauma?" We find the answer in the book of Acts, where we see that the disciples continued to walk in boldness and courage to advance the kingdom of God even as they took some hits. They were thrown into prison, persecuted, wounded, thrown out of cities, and stoned. Yet in the midst of dealing with that trauma, they knew where to go to receive healing and restoration—to Jesus and the Holy Spirit in the context of their larger community.

In Acts 4, right after they were taken before the religious leaders, persecuted, and told not to speak the name of Jesus, they begin to pray. They didn't pray for God to take away their enemies. They prayed for courage, boldness, and the determination to continue to go *in the name of Jesus* to bring the good news to the rest of the world. Then they went forth from there and astounding signs, wonders, and miracles came to the hands of the apostles. That was their destiny and it is yours. To live out your destiny, you need to learn to live with a soul that is experiencing the *shalom* of God.

LIVING IN HOPE

How do we live in the shalom of God? I believe there are indicators that tell you whether or not you are living in the place of shalom. First, in shalom we live in hope—the hope of Jesus returning to restore all things. In the Jesus Movement that occurred in the late 1960s and early 1970s, there was a radical absence of hope. People got saved because they heard the message that Jesus could come back any second, so if they didn't get saved right away they would be left in the hell called earth. That was the message. People were waiting for Jesus to come back any second and would do crazy things like rapture practice. I was in a meeting with an evangelistic group going to Israel. This is when credit cards just became available. We were told that if you wanted to go to Israel, just put the costs on your credit card and pray for the rapture to happen before the bill came due!

The problem that I see with the no-hope message is that I don't believe God wants to do it that way. I don't believe that He wants to take us from this earth so quickly that we leave without understanding that God didn't save us just to go to heaven—He also saved us to bring heaven to earth. I once met a man who built duplexes. He had been so captured by the no-hope message of the Jesus Movement that he built buildings out of the cheapest material possible thinking of them as temporary housing. Guess what happened 30 years later? Those buildings fell apart. This man went to heaven eventually and his sons are dealing with buildings that are falling apart because they were built so badly. That is living without hope.

BELIEVING THE IMPOSSIBLE IS POSSIBLE

A second indicator that you are living in the shalom of God is that the impossible seems reasonable. When the impossible seems possible, God will do the impossible through you. It is possible to live in such a way that you see the miraculous happening every single day of your life because that is what the power of the Holy Spirit puts within us. The very same Spirit who raised Jesus from the grave lives within us. When you live believing that all things are possible in Jesus, you understand that you are predestined to live in the glory of the cross. You wake up every morning acknowledging to God that the impossible seems reasonable. This is part of what it means to live unbroken. The idea of living unbroken is not that you never have problems, but rather that you know the source of healing and restoration.

Romans 8:28-29 says, *"And we know that in all things God works for the good of those who love him, who have been called according to his purpose. For those God foreknew he also predestined to be conformed to the image of his Son, that he might be the firstborn among many brothers and sisters."* No matter what happens to us, He works all things together into the image of Jesus Christ. As ones who bear the image of Christ within us, who is our hope of glory, we are here to bring the hope of transformation to the rest of the world.

> *Father, in Jesus' name we repent on behalf of the church right now. We repent for being so busy building our own buildings and doing our own thing that we haven't see the brokenness in our community. We repent of self-centeredness and pride and*

our own comfort. Forgive us, Lord. Heal us so that we can be a healing conduit to this world. Sow in us Your seeds of hope and the knowledge that all things are possible with You. Lead us to the place of shalom, where, equipped with hope and the faith to believe all things are possible with You, we can go forth into the world as workers in Your great harvest field. In Jesus' name, amen.

NOTE

1. Ehlers A. Clark, DM, "A cognitive model of posttraumatic stress disorder," *Behaviour Research and Therapy* 2000 38(4), abstract, accessed June 9, 2020, https://pubmed.ncbi .nlm.nih.gov/ 10761279.

CHAPTER 3

A BIBLICAL UNDERSTANDING OF TRAUMA

In the Bible there are two scriptures that are foundational to a biblical understanding of trauma. David, who I believe to be one of the most traumatized people in the Bible, declared in Psalm 34:18, *"The Lord is close to the brokenhearted and saves those who are crushed in spirit."* The term *brokenhearted* means "to be shattered into pieces." If you were to take a mirror and throw it on the floor, it would shatter. If you were to look at your face through that shattered mirror, you would see pieces of your face all over. For many people, this is how they respond to trauma—they feel broken on the inside. Because they have been so wounded, they put up walls around their heart, walls of shame and guilt, feeling responsible for what has happened or what they have done. They shelter their broken heart because they don't want any more wounding. They may put on a mask of happiness and function in the world, but the reality is that they are so broken no one ever gets to see their real self because they are sheltered behind the walls they have put up.

Some translations of the Bible refer to the "crushed in spirit" as "contrite in heart or spirit," with the idea of contrite being "I'm sorry for my sin." The root word in Hebrew is "crushed." When you are crushed in this way, the weight of what you've seen or what you carry is so heavy that you feel crushed all the time. I hear testimonies from people who feel crushed by the weight of what they carry without knowing how to get rid of it.

David declares—and this is a wonderful promise—that God is near to the brokenhearted. He saves those crushed in spirit. In Psalm 147:3, David ups the ante and says that God heals the brokenhearted and binds up their wounds. There is a hope and promise that no matter how shattered you are or how much trauma you have been through, God is the God who heals the brokenhearted. He not only heals us; He binds up our hearts too. He brings shattered pieces of our broken heart back together so that we can feel whole again.

As I mentioned earlier, when someone experiences trauma, they can feel what I call "dis-integrated." This means that for them, it feels like the pieces of their mind and heart will never come together again. There is this piece over here and that piece over there, and the pieces never seem to connect. This is dis-integration. The only way re-integration happens to anyone is when Jesus Christ becomes the center of their life.

It says in Colossians 1 that the entire universe is held together through the power of Jesus. Not only did God create the entire universe; He literally sustains the universe, keeping everything together. The inference is that the planets are held in orbit, not by gravity, but the power of Jesus holding things in place. If that is true, then only by His power can we see a re-integration of our lives no matter how broken and chaotic they have become.

Isaiah 61:1-3 has become the bones and structure upon which rests everything I do in ministry.

The Spirit of the Sovereign Lord is on me, because the Lord has anointed me to proclaim good news to the poor. He has sent me to bind up the brokenhearted, to proclaim freedom for the captives and release from darkness for the prisoners to proclaim the year of the Lord's favor and the day of vengeance of our God, to comfort all who mourn, and provide for those who grieve in Zion—to bestow on them a crown of beauty instead of ashes, the oil of joy instead of mourning, and a garment of praise instead of a spirit of despair. They will be called oaks of righteousness, a planting of the Lord for the display of his splendor (Isaiah 61:1-3).

This passage of Scripture is a prophecy about the coming Messiah, Jesus. Isaiah declares that when Messiah comes, this is what He will look like and how you will know that He is in fact the true Messiah. This is fascinating because in Luke 4, Jesus returns to His home synagogue, and one of the first acts of His ministry is to read from Isaiah 61. What a Holy coincidence that the reading that day was Isaiah 61! When He finished reading, He then declared that the scripture had been fulfilled. Jesus began His ministry by declaring that He was the true Messiah. I want you who are reading this right now to understand how you will know Messiah has come.

Isaiah 61:1 says, "The Spirit of God is upon me because the Lord has anointed me." The first thing Jesus tells us is that there is an anointing on His life. Second, He says that He will bring good news to the poor. He will not come to the rich and famous or the religious establishment or heads of government—He will come to the afflicted and the poor. They are His main audience. This is part of the "good news." The word *gospel* means "good news." The next statement Jesus makes is very significant. It doesn't say He will multiply food, get people saved, or cleanse lepers. The identifying mark of the Messiah is this—He has been sent by God to bind up the brokenhearted, bring liberty to captives, and freedom to prisoners. The identifying mark of Messiah is to minister healing to the broken soul of humankind.

Humankind is broken from the trauma of sin, sickness, death, chaos, and hatred. It only makes sense that the primary mission of Jesus in this world is to declare the good news to the afflicted—the good news that He is here to heal broken hearts. He is here to declare freedom to those who have been kidnapped by evil—to set them free and break chains. He is here to declare to those guilty of horrific things that if you have a heart to repent, He will open the prison door and set you free. The power of Jesus the Messiah will set not only captives free, it will even set the guilty free.

Then, in Isaiah 61 Jesus goes on to declare the favorable year of the Lord, the day of vengeance of our God, which is the year of Jubilee in the Jewish calendar. That is the day when everything that had been stolen, everything that had been taken from people was returned to everyone. Those who were sold into slavery because of debt or other reasons were set free from captivity. People in debtor's prison were set free. There is a sense of complete restoration that even if your own choices caused you to fall into captivity or imprisonment, on the Day of Jubilee all is restored in Jesus' name. That is the description of the ministry of Messiah. When we give Him our sin and brokenness, He does a great exchange.

Isaiah 61 begins by telling us of the Lord's favor toward us, then continues by telling us that along with this favor we will receive His comfort:

> *To comfort all who mourn, and provide for those who grieve in Zion—to bestow on them a crown of beauty instead of ashes, the oil of joy instead of mourning, and a garment of praise instead of a spirit of despair. They will be called oaks*

of righteousness, a planting of the Lord for the display of his splendor. They will rebuild the ancient ruins and restore the places long devastated; they will renew the ruined cities that have been devastated for generations (Isaiah 61:2-4).

Instead of mourning your loss, instead of walking in a spirit of grieving and mourning, you receive comfort. There is a reason why Holy Spirit is a comforter. Ultimately, we need comfort from God to heal our trauma and brokenness if we are to step out into unfamiliar places. We need comfort during those times. He gives us comfort instead of mourning, a garland of beauty instead of ashes.

If you recall the story of Job in the Bible, at one point he had lost everything and was covered in boils. He was sitting in a pile of ashes scraping his skin with a broken piece of pottery. That is about as bad as it gets. God tells us that instead of living in the ashes of all that you have lost, He will give you a garland of beauty so that you are not identified by what you have lost, but instead you are identified by what God calls you—and He calls you beautiful. He says He will give you a garment of praise instead of a spirit of heaviness. When people get set free from trauma, they talk about feeling lighter. This feeling of lightness comes because they are no longer carrying the weight of the trauma anymore. People who carry trauma are weighed down. Jesus says that He will lift that weight from us and clothe us in praise. He will shift our identity. We no longer have to live as afflicted. We become oaks of righteousness so that God may be glorified.

LIVING AS OVERCOMERS

As a Baptist, I heard lots of sermons. I'm not against Baptists. I have heard a lot of preaching from Baptists about how God gets glory in our suffering, and that when we suffer for Him God gets glory from our faithfulness. There is a truth in that, but there is also a truth that God gets some of His greatest glory when we are set free from trauma, addiction, pain, and the identity of affliction. When our identity becomes like an oak of righteousness (so that God may be glorified) we are no longer victims or the oppressed. We become victors and overcomers. Instead of being under the enemy's feet, the position is reversed—now the enemy is under our feet. That is how God gets some of the greatest glory on earth.

When you are a "planting of the Lord," not only do you provide shade and comfort and shelter to others, you produce acorns, which produce other oaks. You are no longer multiplying pain and hurt and trauma. Now you are reproducing fruit with seed in it that multiples over and over again. Your greatest weakness becomes your greatest platform for ministry.

Our response to trauma, when viewed through the lens of Scripture, is broken heartedness. I want to highlight three factors that impact how we deal with broken heartedness. The first has to do with our family roots. Many people who experience trauma don't carry it around with them because they have strong family roots. Their family has taught them how to deal with difficult times. They experience a very strong sense of belonging. When you know people really care for you, you have a high level of emotional security. I am an only child. My mom and dad were my biggest cheerleaders. They're both in heaven now, and I know they are standing on the balcony of heaven cheering me on. I grew up secure in who I was in their love. I have been able to walk through trauma in my life because I grew up with a sense of belonging and being loved. People who deal with trauma successfully typically come from strong families.

The second factor has to do with faith. People who are able to handle trauma in healthy ways typically have a strong faith. They walk in faith to such a degree that they can roll pain over onto Jesus. They know the yoke of Jesus is easy and His burden is light. Jesus says, "Come to me you weary, and I will give you rest." The sense of walking in the rest of God in strong faith helps us walk through trauma without it sticking to us.

The third factor that helps us deal with our broken heartedness is the ability to process trauma. Processing is very important. Those who have the ability and opportunity to process trauma right away are much less likely to carry it around with them. They learn how to lay it down right away. We had a young man who was part of our global school who was the sergeant of a crew that would blow up all IEDs in a war zone so the troops could walk on the road safely. This young man had served three tours of duty in war zones. When I questioned him, he didn't seem to have any post-traumatic stress. As we talked, I realized why. He said that at the end of the day he would get his guys together, and no matter who had been injured or what had happened, they would talk about it. They would talk all the trauma out and deal with it instead of carrying it to bed that night.

There is a principle involved in not letting the sun go down on your anger. Dealing with trauma and the emotional responses it produces, no matter what you have been through that day, means rolling it all over to Jesus before you go to bed. When you forgive and release and get cleansed, you can sleep in peace. God designed sleep to regenerate us so that we are ready for each new day. Firefighters and police officers and EMTs who see trauma all the time use these three factors—strong family, faith, and the ability to process the trauma—to stay healthy. In this way they are able to continue to do their jobs. The medical community also employs these three factors to help deal with trauma by getting their team together and debriefing when the work is over for the day. When we have been through something traumatic, we need to debrief with someone. We need to be able to put into words what we have experienced. Women have a grace on them to process in a way that men don't have. Women know how to put words to feelings. Men need to learn how to do this because we have sons and grandsons who need to be raised up in healthy ways. Society has taught us, particularly as men, to suck it up, get over it, stuff it down, and not cry. In Jesus' time, it wasn't just women who carried dead bodies through the streets weeping; it was the men too. That kind of mourning gave everyone an opportunity to get out their grief. When you continue to carry grief, it does harm to your soul and your body.

God provides healing from trauma. If you let Him, He will take the broken pieces of your heart, put them back together, and make you whole. I have seen it happen time and again. This is not just theology; it is reality.

> *Holy Spirit, we welcome Your Presence to fulfill the mission of Jesus according to Isaiah 61:1-3, which says that God sent Jesus to bind up the brokenhearted, to proclaim freedom for captives, and to release prisoners from darkness. Jesus, thank You for a crown of beauty instead of ashes, the oil of joy instead of mourning, and a garment of praise instead of a spirit of despair.*

CHAPTER 4

THE EFFECTS OF TRAUMA ON THE MIND

What is trauma? What does it mean to carry trauma in your life? What does it mean to carry trauma in such a way that it affects your identity, the way you think, feel, and the choices you make? When we look at the biblical definition of trauma, we understand trauma does have things that impact our souls in such a way that even though we are believers in Christ and we are filled with His Spirit, we can still carry memories and the impact of trauma.

From a biblical point of view, I call post-traumatic stress disorder a soul injury. When a person is traumatized, their soul is broken into pieces. The person, according to the tri-partite nature of man, is spirit, soul, and body. When we are talking about the soulish realm, there are three parts—mind, will, emotion. PTSD is an injury to the soul that can only be healed, I believe, by the power of God through prayer.

TRAUMATIC BRAIN INJURY AND PTSD

God created our brain in such a way that all of the memories of what we experience stay with us in the hippocampus. The hippocampus is the memory center of the brain located at the bottom of the brain. Right next to the hippocampus is a gland called the amygdala. The amygdala produces the fight-or-flight hormone. When you experience a threat, your brain must decide whether to stay and fight or take flight. Then there is our brain stem, which sits above our spinal cord and is made up of several parts, including the thalamus and hypothalamus, which are also glands. These two glands serve as relay stations between the spinal cord and the brain, giving direct sensory input to the right place within our cerebral cortex in response to stimuli.

The prefrontal cortex part of the brain is the place that has control of your mind and thus your life. It is the portion of the brain where your most presenting thoughts and your consciousness exist.

The brain has two lobes—a right lobe and a left lobe. The left lobe is considered to be more rational and organized, while the right lobe is considered to be the creative part of the brain. We always talk about being left-brained or right-brained, but the reality is that is not true. We use both sides of our brain on a regular basis. There is something that happens in trauma—when you have been severely traumatized and carry PTSD—where the connections between the left and right lobes of the brain become less active or inactive as a result of trauma. Research shows that connections between the lobes pause when the brain experiences trauma. When this happens, a person will experience a sense of dis-integration because the right and left lobes are not functioning properly. The connection between the lobes is not destroyed by trauma but paralyzed for a period of time.

It is the right lobe of the brain that contains traumatic images as memories, and it is these memories that are the ones that continue to be the most presenting reality in a brain that has experienced trauma. People carry trauma even all the way back to childhood. Traumas that continually impact our adult lives become our present reality. We may be thinking and doing other things, but when we try to use our memory, what happens is we have to go through the access point of those traumatic images and memories. This is why people, particularly veterans and first responders who have experienced a great deal of trauma and have a lot of traumatic memories, end up living those traumatic memories on a daily basis to such a decree that they are their present reality.

Many times, severely traumatized people are unable to remember a lot of good things in life. When you have been severely traumatized, it is as if the traumatic memories highjack your memory system. Your hippocampus does what I call a "coma." Many people with PTSD have a lot of problems with short-term memory loss—they have difficulty remembering where they put their keys or phone, and there are lots of things happening in the short term that they have difficulty remembering.

It is important to understand that PTSD is not a mental illness; it is a psychological injury. In PTSD, the hippocampus shrinks. That is why someone with traumatic images and memories can actually feel as if trauma from five years ago is their present reality. There is increased activity in the amygdala, which is linked to fear responses. The prefrontal cortex, which regulates negative emotions that occur when confronted with stimuli, also shrinks. For example, a brain that is not overtaken by trauma has been trained to control emotions in various situations. Although we may feel fear, we are able to control our fear so that we don't have to run out of the room. If we are confronted by someone who is acting aggressively, our healthy prefrontal cortex may make us feel like we can fight this person, but instead we make the choice not to punch the guy in the nose. That is how a healthy prefrontal cortex works.

For a brain in trauma, those functions are paralyzed, making it very difficult to control emotions. Anxiety and fear increase because of what the brain is telling you about those traumatic images. You get angry and rage for no apparent reason because of what the right lobe of the brain is telling the prefrontal cortex. The traumatized brain is captive to traumatic images and memories.

Sleep disturbances are very typical for those suffering from PTSD, including sleep apnea. Frequent recurrent nightmares make sleep no longer a safe place. When this happens, the brain develops a conditioned response called "fear of sleep." During the day, you have some measure of control over your thoughts, but at night, when the brain is given over to the subconscious, trauma comes rushing back. The result is you really don't like sleeping. People who suffer from trauma-related sleep disorders also have a REM sleep dysregulation. REM sleep is the deepest level of sleep, and is the time when your mind gets refreshed. It is the time you dream the most making it the most restorative portion of your sleep. When a person is unable to go to the REM sleep level because of insomnia and nightmares, they begin to experience excessive motor activity such as restless leg syndrome. They suffer with micro-wakeness, which is when you've just fallen asleep and then you wake up. This keeps happening throughout the night. Micro-wakeness creates a sense of exhaustion because the person never gets the REM sleep they need.

When we pray for someone to be healed of PTSD, we pray for traumatic images in the brain to dry up and die. We command the hippocampus to wake up and function properly and short-term memory to be restored. When these things happen, memory begins to flow once again out of the hippocampus, and the person can remember good things.

I prayed with a woman who had tragically lost an adult daughter in a horrible car accident. She actually saw the accident happen in front of her.

She saw her daughter's lifeless body and all of the awfulness of the accident. When she came to me, she was under a spirit of grieving and mourning that she felt would never leave her. As we began to pray to sever the neuropathways that led to those traumatic images and memories and break the power of pain, the Spirit of God came upon her and began to heal her. Suddenly her posture changed. She had been bent down, almost hunched over as if she had a back issue. As the spirit of God moved on her, her countenance and her posture changed. She started praising and worshiping God, crying uncontrollably. Then her crying moved to laughter as she saw her daughter again for the first time, whole and healed before Jesus. When I spoke with her the next day, she said that the traumatic images were no longer tormenting her; there was no pain attached to them. She told me she had slept for eight hours that night—the first time in two years.

In the gospel of Mark, chapter 11, Jesus spoke to the fig tree that was not producing fruit, commanding it to dry up and die. Our prayers, in the name of Jesus, can accomplish the same thing. The brain is full of neuropathways that look like trees. When we pray and "speak" to the neuropathways that contain traumatic images, we can command them to dry up and die in Jesus' name. We can also pray to sever the trigger points of those images. When we do this, one of two things can happen—either the person will lose the traumatic images and memories, or those images and memories will no longer contain pain.

TRUST GOD FOR YOUR HEALING

If you want to deal with the trauma in your life, it is important that you be able to identify the symptoms. In the process of identifying the symptoms, you may see yourself and get triggered. Please hear me—if you feel yourself being triggered as you read this book, do not be afraid, do not let anxiety or panic overtake you. You are reading this book for a purpose—to be healed and restored. Be assured that God is going to bring His healing over your mind and your soul, and as He does you will come together and be made whole and trauma will come off your life.

People react to trauma in a variety of ways, with trauma symptoms varying in intensity over time. You may have more symptoms when stressed in general or when reminded of whatever it was you experienced that is causing you trauma. For example, let's say you were in a car accident that left you so traumatized that every time you get in a car, it triggers that trauma making it difficult for you to drive. Just getting in the car may also trigger memories of pain in your body. Or, perhaps you were in a car accident and although there was some trauma attached to it, that experience has caused you to learn to be a better driver so that when you get in a car, you are reminded to drive well rather than being rendered almost unable to drive. We all respond in a variety of ways depending on circumstances. There is no one blueprint for how we respond to trauma.

I was in a car accident in Los Angles with an Uber driver outside LAX airport. We were riding in a Kia Soul, which is not a very large car. The Uber driver rear-ended the car in front of us that was lined up in a line of cars. We were going 50 miles per hour. I was in the back seat and thankfully God protected me. I was okay and I even made my flight. The next time I was in a car being driven somewhere—and how many of you know there is a difference between driving and riding—when the driver would get close to the car in front of us, I would feel triggered. Realizing what was going on, I prayed, "Lord, I know what this is. Bring healing to the memory of that trauma so I no longer feel that sense of going into fear and panic." Thanks be to God; He brought His healing to me in that moment. He will do the same for you. God will heal you. Ask

Him into your heart, ask people to pray for you, and receive God's healing.

> *Jesus, I welcome You to come heal all trauma in my life. Thank You for laying down Your life so that I can be free. Thank You that the finished work of the cross is absolutely and completely sufficient to cleanse me and make me new so that I may live fully in my identity as Your beloved son or daughter.*

CHAPTER 5

The Schemes of Satan to Torment the Traumatized

John 10:10 tells us that *"the thief comes only to steal and kill and destroy."* This is nowhere more evident than in trauma. Yet the remainder of this verse brings us God's answer to the devil's schemes: *"I have come that they may have life, and have it to the full."* While much scientific research has been done regarding trauma and how to treat the traumatized, it is my experience that true and complete healing from trauma comes from Jesus. There is a holistic healing that only Jesus can bring to a soul that has been shattered, through reintegration of all of the shattered pieces in the power of the Spirit of God. I am not advocating that people stop seeking medical help. I believe that trauma sufferers can benefit from treatments available today from the medical community *and* from healing in Jesus Christ; the two can go hand in hand. This book focuses on the healing that is found in Jesus.

THE SCHEMES OF THE DEVIL

The devil is the thief who comes to kill, steal, and destroy, and he does this in a variety of ways. The following are some of the ways I have seen the devil torment the traumatized.

Victim Mentality

The symptoms of trauma can be so unrelenting and so distressing that some who suffer from trauma have a tendency to talk about their trauma constantly. This is because, when a person's soul is shattered, the traumatic things that have happened to them become their identity. They begin to believe the truest thing about them is the fact that they are a victim, which causes them to tell their story over and over again. This identity as a victim and the constant revisiting of trauma will eventually cement the plan of the enemy to steal, kill, destroy the dream of God for that person's life. It brings one to a place where their identity is not who they are in God, but in the way the enemy has sought to destroy the dream God has for them.

Thanks to Jesus, we are no longer defined by our history. We are not defined by what has been done to us, or what has not been done to us, or by the choices that we have made. We are truly defined by who God calls us to be—His beloved children in whom He is well pleased.

Worry

Worrying accomplishes nothing while stealing the life right out of us. When we worry and are full of fear about what is coming or what may happen or take place, we are listening to a demon spirit that is lying and wants us to believe that the worst is yet to come. For example, if I were to go and find a flat tire on my car, and the first thing out of my mouth is, "Well, of course," I am living with a mindset that expects bad things to happen in my life. That kind of a mindset has its basis in worry. Oftentimes a person doesn't know they have this kind of mindset because it is so deeply ingrained in their thinking.

The devil is the author of worry. God is the author of hope and peace. When I repent and change the way I think and believe God is big enough to take care of me and watch over me, I can live with a heavenly mindset and not a hellish mindset. Why live with a hellish mindset? Why not choose to live with a heavenly mindset that says you are not alone, you are provided for and have nothing to fear? To be free of worry, you have to kick worrisome thinking to the trash and pick up hope. When we have hope, we can begin to walk in peace. You do not have to let the spirit of worry and fear access your mind. The choice is yours. You can choose to think the devil's thoughts or God's thoughts. If you are ready to think God's thoughts, make this simple declaration with me:

> *God has not given me a spirit of fear, of anxiety, or worry. God has given me power, love, and a sound mind. I do not need to worry or be anxious. Fear is not part of me. I have a sound mind because I have the mind of Christ. Therefore, I think God's thoughts and my mind is at peace.*

Strongholds of Lies

Second Corinthians 10:3-5 talks about destroying strongholds and casting down speculations and every lofty thing that raises itself against the knowledge of God. The devil tries to set up strongholds of lies and speculations and all kinds of seemingly lofty things that he wants us to exalt above the things of God. I see these strongholds often in those with a history of trauma. When we have a stronghold full of lies based upon traumatic experiences, it not only impacts and speaks to our present, it also speaks to our future causing us to live with a mental stronghold that says that because of our past history we can only expect bad things to happen to us in the future. With this kind of thinking, we are always waiting for the next bad thing to happen. Our imagination and speculation is not positive but negative, which affects our hope, our faith, and how we believe our future will be. What needs to be torn down are the imaginations and speculations that are based upon the history of our trauma. It is this history of our trauma that causes us to walk in unbelief and a lack of faith and trust in God.

A woman who was struggling with a stronghold of lies that kept her from receiving full healing from traumatic memories attended a conference where I was speaking. Prior to the conference, she felt the Lord tell her that if she went He would meet her there. Although she had walked through much inner healing, she would still cry herself to sleep at night because of the tormenting memories in her head. She was losing hope and was in a place where she thought she "just had to deal with it." Believing the lie that because she was a survivor and therefore an overcomer, she had been living with a "just deal with it" mindset. She reasoned that others had suffered much worse than she had, and because her suffering was "minor" she just needed to buck up and keep going.

As she sat in the conference listening to me teach on PTSD, she began to recognize herself. As the stronghold of lies began running through her head once again, she remembered how the Lord had told her He would meet her at the conference. Sensing that this was the moment of their meeting, she became open to what God was doing. No one prayed for her, no one laid hands on her; she didn't interact with anyone. God just began to heal her as she sat there. Overcome, she wept in surrender, astonishment, and gratitude as His presence rested upon her. When she opened her eyes, all the colors in the room were brighter; everything appeared crystal clear to her. Even so, she could tell that something was still clinging to her, so she came forward and asked me for prayer.

As Holy Spirit gave me discernment concerning the trauma and the stronghold of lies in her life, I asked her to start declaring Kingdom thoughts over herself. She said afterward that she felt a physical release over her tongue as if the enemy had been forbidding her to speak God's truth over herself. As she spoke the words, God's peace descended on her as a heavy weight on her shoulders. She has walked in freedom since, in the joy of the Lord. She now understands that she had mistakenly taken responsibility for some things that had happened in the life of her family that were not hers in the first place. In doing so she had opened the door for those things to attach to her. When she was able to lay down those things and sever those soul ties, the torment-ing memories dried up and left her.

In the past, when she had received healing, she had fallen prey to the lie that full healing wasn't pos-sible because the torment would return. As a result, she lived in survivor mode instead of conqueror mode. God broke those lies off her and she now walks in freedom, continuing to declare and speak His truths over herself as she walks in deeper levels of freedom.

Loss of God-Given Identity

Each one of us is created in the image and like-ness of God (see Gen. 1:27). Some of us don't know that truth because the devil is always looking for ways to rob us of our true identity. Are you in the habit of always criticizing yourself, always demeaning yourself, living life afraid that one day people will find out that you aren't really a good person? If so, you might have lost your God-given identity. God intends that you like yourself and even love yourself. How else can you love others and love God unless you love the person who God created you to be? God intends that you live in shalom, waking up every morning and saying, "God loves me, He is here for me, and therefore I will love myself."

There are three things that repentance means for me. It means that I have to change the way I think about God, the way I think about what is available to me, and ultimately the way I think about myself. If you have thoughts in your mind that cause you to demean and criticize yourself, to live in fear that others will think badly of you, you need to repent. You need to start believing what God says about you—that you are loved and loveable. You need to love yourself the way God loves you. Sometimes that takes a prayer that says, "God, help me to see myself the way You see me. Help me to know that You love me, and that You will not abandon me or forsake me."

Identity is a significant issue for those suffering from trauma. Whatever your identity was before the trauma, afterward your identity changes. Military service can compound an already skewed identity. Many young men and women go into the military at a young age, right out of high school. One of the primary reasons is because they are escaping dysfunctional family environments. They come out of these environments without a good identity. They may come out of places of rage, pain, abuse, and dysfunction into the military, and the first identity they get is that of a soldier or military person. That becomes their identity. One of the first things they do in the military is break down your identity as a civilian and build it up as a solider. That is great as long as you are in the military, but when you step out as a veteran, while you carry the title "veteran," a veteran is a badge of honor but is not a functional identity in this world.

The reason why post-traumatic stress gets worse for so many veterans is, the further they get away from the military the greater their loss of identity. The sense of loss of identity and purposelessness creates even more if an issue, especially for men. Men primarily identify themselves by what they do. Here is what one veteran actually wrote about his loss of identity:

> Who am I? I look in the mirror and it still looks like me, but it doesn't feel like me. Who is this empty person who looks like

me? I have days that I can barely get out of bed, thoughts keep flashing through my head. Why won't it stop? Get up, get over it, pull yourself together. Ah, what is wrong with me? My family doesn't get me, they don't hear me, they only see the outside, the shell that looks like me. Where is the person who occupied this empty shell? I know I am still in here beneath the pain and despair. I am stuck in hell inside my own head, living in the past, but the past is right now. I can't make it stop, no matter how hard I try. I am broken and shattered. Who am I?

JESUS HAS ALL AUTHORITY

One of the things that exacerbates these kinds of identity issues is the culture of victimhood we now live in, which I mentioned earlier. Today's culture tells us that we can excuse every bad thing about us because we are victims. What you end up with are people who identify more with trauma than with the good things they have experienced in life. When I pray for people with trauma, I don't want to hear about all of the trauma. Some trauma victims get something out of regurgitating all of the trauma in their life. They are more than happy to tell you all the bad things. Something happens in their mind that they get a payoff out of their trauma whether it be self-pity, victimhood, or whatever it is. That becomes their identity, and they want to impress you and intimidate you with the trauma that they have experienced.

I have instances of ministering to someone who has suffered satanic ritual abuse, where they will try to intimidate me and let me know that no one has been more traumatized than they are—that their trauma is so deep and strong that no one can do anything about it. When I encounter this, I look them in the eye and say, "If you believe in Jesus and trust Him, He will heal you no matter how bad your trauma is." And I always smile at them. I don't care how horrendous their past behavior is or what has been done to them. I always smile and say, "If you want to, you can be free of this today in Jesus' name." I do not let what is on them overwhelm me because I know that "greater is He who is in me than is in the world." That is the crux of healing in Jesus' name. Jesus has all authority, and "all" means all!

We live in a disposable culture. The Japanese are not that way. They have an art form called *kintsugi*, which is their way of recognizing beauty in broken-ness. Kintsugi artists take a vessel that is broken and repair it by gluing the pieces back together with dust mixed with silver, gold, or platinum. When they put the vessel back together, it is actually more beautiful and more valuable for having been broken. This is a perfect picture of the ministry of Jesus. He comes to heal the brokenhearted, bind up their wounds, bring shattered pieces back together, and bring freedom to captives and prisoners, to make a broken person a vessel of honor in the household. Jesus brings beauty from ashes (see Isa. 61:3).

Someone once asked me if some people were created as vessels of dishonor versus honor. My answer is no. When we start out without Jesus, we are all destined to be vessels of dishonor. With Jesus we all have potential to be vessels of honor. No matter how bad or sinful we are, when Jesus comes into our life, He takes broken pieces and uses the gold of His kingdom to put us together so that we become vessels of honor in His house.

UNFORGIVENESS AND OFFENSE

The devil loves to stir up a spirit of offense and unforgiveness in people's lives and this is very evident in the traumatized. The spirit of offense is rife even in the church. We have all seen those who become offended at the least little thing and carry that offense around so that everyone who comes near must tiptoe by with great care so as not to aggravate that touchy spirit. Offense and unforgiveness go hand in hand. To forgive and refuse to be offended is to strong-arm bitterness. Pushing back against bitterness is a decision that needs to be made every day, no matter what happens, no matter how others treat you. It is an offensive strategy, not a defensive posture.

Forgiveness and that which goes along with it destroys victimhood. It makes you the opposite of a victim. Forgiveness makes you an overcomer who is in control of every situation that comes your way. Say, for instance, you go to work and get a message from the boss that indicates a negative encounter between the two of you is about to take place. If you got up that morning and made the decision afresh to forgive and forego offense no matter what the situation, the spirit of offense will not have control over you when you walk into your boss' office and interact with him or her. We cannot control others' behavior, but we can control ours. Because you are not thinking like a victim, you can go into life's situations and walk in peace within yourself regardless of the storm around you.

FEAR AND TIMIDITY

Many people, especially those struggling with trauma, have a problem with boldness. Boldness is not an issue of one being an introvert or extrovert; it is not about personality. Boldness is how much you believe God is for you. Courage and boldness come from believing God is with you and then stepping out and believing that what He told you to do, you can do and He will back you up. If God is for you, who can be against you?

When our confidence is solely in our own wisdom and our own skills and abilities, we are going to experience failure. Even the most successful person will eventually come up against something that causes them to fail. Because successful people have been so self-reliant, failure can be especially hard for them. Personal failure can bring a lack of confidence and can lead to fearfulness and even timidity, where we feel weak and ineffective. There is nothing wrong with being confident in your own skills and abilities. The mistake is thinking you are the be all and end all. Trauma that makes you feel out of control, worthless, and victimized can bring a mindset that even God can't overcome what is going on in your life. That is a lie.

Here is the testimony of a woman who was healed at one of Global Awakening's conferences when she was willing to surrender control and trust God for her healing:

I was a victim of child abuse, witchcraft, and sorcery. My stepmother would cut locks of my hair to practice voodoo. In my late teens I joined the military and served for ten years in special operations. I had to retire at 100 percent disability due to PTSD. I was told by doctors that there was no cure for my trauma. I would pray for deliverance and have moments when I would feel God's presence, but no healing. I prayed and prayed for Jesus to show me what to do. Eventually I came to realize that I needed to surrender control. I had been trying to "soldier" through the trauma on my own but it wasn't working. No one can fix their own brokenness. Only Jesus can heal. When I was willing to let go of control and become vulnerable, I received healing and deliverance. Even though I was triggered at first by the idea of stepping into a vulnerable place, once I allowed myself to be prayed for, I received healing. It was a divine appointment. I just want to say that Jesus loves you so much.

In Second Corinthians 12, Paul talks about all the things he has been through that have led him to the realization that he has a thorn in the flesh that causes him to cry out to God. I believe this refers to someone persecuting him. Paul tells us that God's message is that when we are weak He displays His strength in the most beautiful way. The greatest thing I learned about God is that when He called me He already factored in my weakness. He knew everything about me and yet He still called me. Why? Because God knows that when I am weak, when I fail, He is there to back me up, to pick me up. When I understand that—when I am living for Him and the things I am doing are for Him—I can be courageous because God is backing me up. My confidence is God, not my ability.

CRITICAL SPIRIT

Often the enemy manifests as a critical spirit in those struggling with trauma. We are all called according to what the scriptures say, and scripture says that we are to encourage one another (see 1 Thess. 5:11). To encourage one another is literally to give courage, to say to people that it is okay to be who you are—to give others encouragement to be their authentic self. The lie of religion says that if people knew who you really were, they would reject you. Anything that is attached to shame or guilt or sin has already been buried with Jesus Christ—nailed on the cross and buried. Therefore, our authentic self is not the sin that we may have committed; it is not our past. When we are in Jesus Christ, we are a new creation. The old is passed away, all things are new (see 2 Cor. 5:17).

In the midst of this realization comes the ability to say that no matter what is going on, we can encourage others and call out the gold in them. It is easy to see the dirt in someone's life, but it takes a person with God's sight to find the gold in others, seeing them with the eyes of Jesus, with the fullness of who they are as their authentic selves. Jesus will cast out the critical spirit in you and replace it with His Spirit. When the Spirit of the living God is in you, you will hear Him speaking words of healing, love, and affirmation over your life. If you are hearing anything else, you are not hearing God's Spirit.

BREAKING THE POWER OF THE ENEMY

Your destiny, your purpose in this life is to glorify God with the shalom of God upon you. If there is anything in your heart that has been exposed by God, I break the power of shame off of you now in the name of Jesus. I break the power of guilt off of you now in the name of Jesus. There is no condemnation in Christ Jesus. God is not calling you to live by laws or rules or things you can never attain. The spirit of life has set you free. When you find yourself lacking, pray this short prayer:

> *Holy Spirit help me! You know my weakness; You know where I lack. Help me, Holy Spirit, to be like the lame man at the gate beautiful, where I receive Your healing, Your transformation, and Your freedom in my life. Amen.*

CHAPTER 6

GOD'S HEART TO RESTORE AND HEAL THE TRAUMATIZED

In these days we are in, Father God is calling forth you and all of His sons and daughters to walk in wholeness according to His original intention for our lives. He is calling each one of us by our true God-given name, which is "beloved." You are treasured, favored, and one who pleases God's heart because He made you that way. No matter what you have been through, no matter how you have reacted to your life and the ways in which people have treated you, God's thoughts and feelings about you have not changed. You are precious in His sight, so precious that He sent His only Son to rescue you from the bondage of the enemy.

So often, particularly in western culture, we think that if we just have the right formula or the right tool it will change everything for us—fix all our problems. I have a master's degree in pastoral counseling and I'm all about training for skills and learning prayer models and ways to minister to people, but ultimately it is about Jesus healing His bride. It is about the power of the Holy Spirit who comes alongside us as the comforter and who takes care of everything needed to restore our soul.

When David wrote Psalm 23, he made a declaration about the identity of the Lord Jesus as the Shepherd who restores our souls to such an extent that we shall not want for anything. What this tells me is that David experienced what it was to have a soul that needed restoring, to have a soul that needed help, and that he also experienced God's restoration. How else could he have made a statement about our soul being restored so completely that we shall want for nothing? You don't come to that kind of conclusion outside of personal experience.

Most of us have walked around at one time or another with brokenness in our soul. The Bible talks about brokenness as a high value for a life that expresses itself in humility. Countless sermons have been preached about how God wants to break us or use us as broken vessels. The problem is that in a lot of teaching, it is hard to determine the difference between what God is doing with regard to brokenness and what the enemy has done to break and destroy our souls. There is a big difference. If we are walking around with brokenness of soul and we think God did this to us, that God caused this brokenness, then it is hard to trust Him to heal us of anything.

HE SETS THE CAPTIVES FREE

So many of us are believers and love Jesus, but we have this stuff in our souls and lives that we think is part of who we are, part of our identity. When we carry bondages for a long time, we begin to believe the enemy's lies that our bondages are our identity. We walk around with all this broken heartedness and don't realize that so much of what captivates us and holds us in bondage to feelings of shame and guilt is not part of who we are. Many of us have been told by people in our life that our brokenness is our identity, but that is a lie of the enemy. God our Father does not see us as traumatized, addicted, sinful, bad, shameful, or guilty. God sees us the way He created us to be—whole, healthy, and free from the bondage of the devil.

You have a spirit, a soul, and a physical body. Your spirit is where the Holy Spirit comes in and joins with you; it is where your mind, will, and emotions come together to make up your soul. The promise of Jesus the Messiah was to bring good news to the poor, the demonized, and the victimized. He demonstrated this good news through healing the brokenhearted—those whose souls were broken from their experiences.

I graduated from seminary, got married, and we moved to southern Illinois to do full-time ministry in a parsonage church. I was taking every tool that I had learned in seminary and pouring it out as a pastor in my Baptist church. I was planning to show them what an amazing pastor I was and how skilled I was because I thought getting a master's degree and being ordained as a Baptist pastor would take care of my own soul issues. That was a lie. I had some strongholds and thoughts that I had carried going back to childhood. I carried all of that into my pastoral ministry. As long as things were going smoothly for me, I was able to put all that stuff in a back corner of my life. It wasn't until I began to experience failures in my ministry and my life that my brokenness came out.

Over the years I have ministered to many people who are looking for hope—hope that there is something that can change inside of them and then everything will be alright. This false notion of hope comes from a demonic, lying spirit that breeds helplessness and hopelessness. When my brokenness emerged, I found myself in a war zone. Every morning when I woke up, I was in a war over the dream of God for my life, and that war was seeking to kill, steal, and destroy what God had promised me as a beloved son. When I began to wake up to that reality, I realized that the sins, temptations, and lies that had wrapped themselves around my soul were not part of who I really was. I tried but couldn't go on faking it until I made it, trying to act holy when I was miserable and tormented on the inside.

LIVING AS BELOVED SONS AND DAUGHTERS

Bill Johnson teaches about how Jesus is perfect theology. He likes to say that anything we think about God that is not found in Jesus needs to be examined, because Jesus is the perfect representation of the Father. When we begin to think about God in terms of who He is as a father, we realize that we have got to get ourselves focused on who God really is *as Jesus has revealed Him to be*. And it follows that we then need to see ourselves in that same light. God is calling His sons and daughters to step out of a place of slavery to our flesh, our experiences, and our desires and step into the place of being His beloved heirs.

So many of us have been born into families with pain and dysfunction. Jesus died so that we don't have to live with addiction for the rest of our days. We don't have to live with the kind of urges that make us feel ashamed and guilty. We don't have to live under a curse any longer. We can be free in Jesus' name. Even though my family came from a background of insanity, alcoholism, and suicide, Jesus Christ came and met me and saved me. He set me free and redeemed my entire family too. Whenever I hear of a Christian leader who has fallen in immorality, there is no judgment in my soul toward them. I only weep because I know what it is like to be that pastor who is preaching the message of salvation and righteousness, and speaking to my people about being holy before God, and then going home on Sunday night crying out before God saying, "I can't get rid of these thoughts in my head, this hopelessness, this broken heartedness."

The Bible likens our lives to a jar of clay in the potter's hand, the potter being God. The good news is that Jesus died on the cross for every broken heart and every broken soul—for every shattered life. He is the only one who can put the pieces of our shattered lives back together. God already sees the victory over your life because of what Jesus did on the cross. He is calling you to take your focus off your shame, guilt, and condemnation and focus instead on what is right in Jesus Christ. You can walk in the righteousness of Christ, and when you do you will leave self-hate behind.

We have difficulty experiencing God's love not because He is holding out on us, but because of the obstacles in our own mind that keep us from seeing ourselves as God sees us. During the years that I struggled with my own issues, I was unable to look myself in the eye in the mirror because I felt such shame and guilt for all the things I had done and was doing. I felt like such a hypocrite that I couldn't experience God's love. What you need to understand is that God has already made a decision about you. He loves you, no matter what. What you do from this moment on is not dependent upon the quality or quantity of His love for you. God has already chosen to love you with an everlasting love that will never fail, and a commitment to see you become the very best of the dream He had for you when you were first conceived in your mother's womb. All of the sin, all the addictions and lies have already been dealt with by God through Jesus on the cross. God has made His decision about you; He has decided in your favor. All you have to do is step into the truth of what God says about you.

The following testimony is from a man we will call Gene who was healed of trauma:

> When I was a combat medic, I had heat stroke and was injured by lightning. During that time, I developed fibromyalgia, which was debilitating. I ended up losing my income because I couldn't work. A whole lot of thoughts were in my head. The depression was very much a struggle. There were thoughts of suicide, worthlessness, the pain was constant. It put a strain on my marriage. I really didn't have a lot of hope. You go from being a man of action, constantly helping people, to zero and you wonder where am I going with this? Where is God in this? You get lost. I had done a good job of trying to suck it up and be quiet and not talk to people about my problems. At first, I was whining and complaining, "Where is God in this? I love God and God doesn't do these

things, but yet here I am. Here I am hurting and bitter." I hurt in my heart.

Friends of mine said I could really use some help. They thought I could benefit from deliverance prayer. I had been a lifelong Christian, led people to Christ, and I thought I had an understanding of how that worked, and I wasn't comfortable with deliverance. My friends directed me to someone named John, who asked how I was doing. I said fine, but Holy Spirit told John, "No, he needs to talk." When John prayed for me, I didn't expect healing. I told John I wasn't comfortable and didn't believe in healing. I knew God and Jesus could heal, but this wasn't something that happened, not a church thing.

Then something connected with me saying healing was real and good and so I got prayer help. Through prayer I began to experience freedom as an intense feeling of relief. The first day after I got prayer, I woke up and realized I didn't feel as sore as usual. I thought it was just a good day; it happens every once in a while. I'd be free of pain for a day only to have it come back. I tried many things to get rid of the pain—neurological drugs, exercise. But that day after prayer I felt different, better than even a normal day. My healing has stood the test of time, and the fibromyalgia is gone.

Before I was healed, I have gone years helping lead people to God and yet I doubted that He could walk in and say, "This isn't my plan for your life." There was guilt associated with my trauma. Through more prayer I let that guilt go, and that was extremely freeing. There was no longer shame for me, no guilt, no negative feelings anymore. God always had plans for me and He loves me and cares for me.

When you see yourself through the eyes of God, it is huge because there is nothing greater than seeing who you really are through His eyes and the love He has for you and the plans He has for you, and everything took place because it needed to, and He has got you. It was really hard being a person of action who takes control of situations and then being helpless.

Through prayer for healing I learned that it's okay, it's all right, it's a struggle, but God is good in the struggle. He never had any intention of letting things be as they were. I can promise you that greater is God in me than was in my world because that old traumatized guy I once was hasn't been back.

RESTORING THAT WHICH WAS LOST

As I mentioned before, our first-world western culture tends to be a throw-away culture. If something stops working, we just throw it away and get another one instead of fixing what was broken. Even in the church, when people quit working the way they are supposed to work and don't live up to our expectations, we have a tendency to throw them away or at least avoid them so that they are not part of our lives anymore. The kingdom of God is not a throw-away culture. Jesus makes all things new. He takes broken people and puts us back together again so that we can live as God intends. The covenant blessing of God for His people is His promise of shalom—of wholeness in every area of our lives.

The book of Nehemiah is a beautiful picture of God coming back to Jerusalem, a city that once had His presence and power. It was the jewel of the earth, but because the people God planted in that city turned away from Him to worship idols, eventually the hordes came against the city and destroyed it. All of the walls that protected the city were torn down, enabling the enemy to come and go freely. Nehemiah, who was not living in Jerusalem at the time, heard about the devastation of the city, and as a man of God he wept over the report of what was happening in Jerusalem. God put it in his heart to go back there and begin to rebuild the city so as to restore it back to the jewel it once was.

One of the very first things Nehemiah did was rebuild the wall around Jerusalem. He rebuilt the wall with burnt stones that had been knocked out of the wall during the destruction of the city. Nehemiah took the burnt stones and used them to rebuild the wall, which is a picture of how God rebuilds our broken souls.

GOD'S INVITATION FOR YOU

God is inviting you to enter into the dream He has for your life in a fresh way. It begins by embracing God's truth that you are the righteousness of God in Jesus Christ. This is how God sees you and how He wants you to see yourself. He is eagerly waiting to put the shattered pieces of your life back together as He restores your soul. His goodness and mercy are running after you every day of your life with His invitation to be His beloved who dwells in His house forever.

King David wrote Psalm 23 as a way to metaphorically express his understanding of the Lord as the good shepherd who lovingly cares for His flock, keeping us safe and providing for our physical and spiritual needs. God's goodness and grace are evident in every line of Psalm 23. Receive God's invitation to walk with Him right now through His green pastures, to rest beside His still waters, to walk the path of righteousness He has for you. He is inviting you to sit at the table He has set in the presence of your enemies and marvel at how He heals you and invites you to receive His spirit of adoption so that you may live in freedom with Him now and forever.

> *The Lord is my shepherd: I shall not want.*
> *He makes me lie down in green pastures.*
> *He leads me beside still waters. He restores*
> *my soul. He leads me in paths of righteous-*
> *ness for his name's sake. Even though I walk*
> *through the valley of the shadow of death, I*
> *will fear no evil, for you are with me; your*
> *rod and your staff, they comfort me. You*
> *prepare a table before me in the presence*

of my enemies; you anoint my head with oil; my cup overflows. Surely goodness and mercy shall follow me all the days of my life, and I shall dwell in the house of the Lord forever (Psalm 23 ESV).

CHAPTER 7

UNDERSTANDING GOD'S GIFT OF FREEDOM

People have a lot of definitions for the word *freedom*. How many remember the movie *Braveheart*? It tells the story of William Wallace, a Scottish commoner who led a rebellion against the tyrannical King Edward I of England. Wallace wasn't about fighting. He wanted a good family life, but the oppressor who came against the nation of Scotland affected him in a deeply personal way, stealing the dream of God for his life. He came to a place where he realized he needed to lead his people to freedom even though it cost him his life. Some parts of the movie are difficult to watch, but it is about people hungry for freedom. Are you hungry for freedom? Are you willing to forgo your own freedom for the sake of those around you, in Jesus' name?

RECEIVE THE SPIRIT OF ADOPTION

Today is the greatest day in human history to harvest souls for Jesus Christ. We have great resources and great outpourings of God's love and power throughout the earth. There are more people to save, heal, deliver, and set free than have ever been at any other time in history. To participate in this great harvest is a privilege available to all of us. I have a personal belief based on Hebrews 12 that all of the men and women of God—the apostles, prophets, evangelists, pastors, teachers, the 12 disciples, the prophets from the Old Testament, Adam and Eve, all of the great women of God and the forefathers who came before us like Martin Luther, John Calvin, William Seymour—all are standing at the balcony of heaven looking down at us saying, "Go for it, church! We prayed for this day, we fasted for this day. We want to be on earth now with what you get to walk in." Even though they are enjoying their reward in heaven, they are excited about what is available for us now that was not available to them. As my friend Tom Jones says, "Why not here, why not now, why not us?"

In Romans 8, the apostle Paul is writing to the Roman church, a church he has never met. He begins chapter 8 with the amazing declaration that there is no condemnation for those in Christ Jesus, for the spirit of life has set us free from the law of the sin of death. A little further along Paul talks of our special relationship with God—that we are children of God:

> *For those who are led by the Spirit of God are the children of God. The Spirit you received does not make you slaves, so that you live in fear again; rather, the Spirit you received brought about your adoption to sonship. And by him we cry, "Abba, Father"* (Romans 8:14-15).

One of Father God's messages to us, His children, is the message of freedom found in the spirit of adoption. God wants His sons and daughters to know that we can be free to be His children. *"Yet to all who did receive him, to those who believed in his name, he gave the right to become children of God"* (John 1:12). It is important to understand that God has a purpose for this freedom. The apostle Paul references this purpose: *"It is for freedom that Christ has set us free"* (Gal. 5:1). The prophet Isaiah explains Paul's reference:

> *The Spirit of the Sovereign Lord is on me, because the Lord has anointed me to proclaim good news to the poor. He has sent me to bind up the brokenhearted, to proclaim freedom for the captives and release from darkness for the prisoners* (Isaiah 61:1).

As we become free in Christ, we can lead others to that same freedom.

TRUE FREEDOM

We have been saved and set free for a purpose beyond ourselves. However, before we can move in that purpose, it is important that you and I understand what real freedom is and what freedom is actually available to us. It is important that we understand that there are counterfeits to freedom that have been propagated by a religious spirit in the church and a spirit of rebellion, particularly in the American culture. Let me explain what I mean. I grew up in the 1960s, in a time when there was a breaking off of the shackles of what some considered to be burdens on their personal freedoms.

These so-called burdens were actually the societal norms that formed the moral fabric of the culture regarding what is right, just, and pure.

I believe that this move toward "freedom" was fueled by the demonic spirit that led a whole generation of people into lives of illicit sex, drugs, and addictions, causing millions of ruined lives. Eventually that very same spirit, I believe, led to the 1973 decision by the Supreme Court to make abortion legal in this country, causing millions of babies to be aborted. People called it freedom, but their notion of freedom came with a skewed definition. The kind of freedom they were pursuing has nothing free about it. The very things they were embracing—illicit sex, drugs, addiction, and abortions—led to more chains, shackles, and burdens that destroy lives. This is a picture of the plan of the evil one to steal, kill, and destroy the dream of God for every life. When we understand there indeed are counterfeits to freedom, we can understand the importance of getting definitions right.

COUNTERFEIT DEFINITIONS FOR FREEDOM

There are three counterfeit definitions for freedom that I want to explore as laid out by Bob Hamp in his book *Think Differently Live Differently: Keys to a Life of Freedom.*[1]

Absence of Boundaries

Living with no boundaries is a counterfeit definition of freedom. Scripture tells us to *"enter through the narrow gate. For wide is the gate and broad is the road that leads to destruction, and many enter through it"* (Matt. 7:13). The premise of life with no boundaries is that if I live without any constraints on my life then I am free to be who I want to be and do what I want to do. The problem with this counterfeit definition is that God Himself established boundaries for the human race, and the reason why is not because He is a mean, angry God or a vengeful God. God established boundaries for His people so that they would know blessing and could be free and protected.

I don't know much about horses, but I know a few people who do. When you try to train a wild horse, you begin by putting it in a corral and letting it find the boundaries. Once that horse finds the boundaries, no matter how wild, they will eventually settle down and can become more easily trainable because they feel safe within the boundaries of the corral. We trust God, but we still lock our doors and our cars at night because that is good stewardship. We don't do these things out of fear.

We do these things because we are called by God to establish boundaries. The idea of freedom being an absence of boundaries is a lie of the enemy.

A healthy person has boundaries. Healthy relationships have boundaries. How many of you know people who want to constantly violate your boundaries, who want you to be on demand for them? Some of us have family members who are in the snare of the devil, causing us to sometimes set boundaries for those family members. My wife and I have healthy boundaries with each other. I know what not to mess with when it comes to her things. Sometimes she will say to me, "Mike, would you go into my purse and get this or that." My response is to say, "No, here comes your purse, you get it." I set that boundary because I know what is going to happen. I will go rummaging around in her purse looking for something only to have her tell me later what a mess I made of her purse. I just don't get in the purse to begin with. That's my boundary.

Absence of Frustrating Habits

There is a second counterfeit definition of freedom that says freedom is the absence of frustrating habits. According to this definition of freedom, we get focused on treating the symptoms of what is happening with us instead of dealing with the root cause. It goes something like this: "If I could just quit drinking, or smoking, or eating the way that I do, everything would be better." This is treating symptoms as if they're the main issue regarding our freedom. The idea is that if you can just quit doing something—cursing, gossiping, lying—then everything will be better.

There are plenty of therapists, psychologists, and self-help books to train us to quit bad habits. There are hypnotists who try to get people to stop smoking and cognitive behavior techniques to try and bring about behavioral change when the reality is that true freedom only comes when you deal with the root cause of your bondage. The church is guilty in this regard. Preachers get up on stage and give us five ways to live a healthier life, ten steps to quit eating so much, seven ways to get rid of an addictive habit, and so on and so on. It is all about what you and I can do to get our own freedom.

Here's the problem—any freedom that I get for myself is always going to be counterfeit. Only one person is willing to pay the price for my freedom, and His name is Jesus. Whenever I am able to overcome something without Jesus' help, without declaring my weakness and allowing His strength to come into me, then I am doing my own thing and not depending on Him. That was the sin of Adam and Eve, to live life independent of God, and it is a strategy that does not work. When we allow God to heal the root cause of our issues, true freedom follows.

Lack of True Identity

The third counterfeit definition of freedom is that if circumstances or relationships change then your problems will go away. Perhaps your job feels like bondage, or your marriage, and you keep thinking that if only you had a better job or a promotion, if only you were married to someone else then you would be happy. If only your circumstances would change then you would be free. This kind of thinking is not a pathway to freedom; it is a lie. When you think this way, you are actually walking in bondage.

Freedom is the ability to respond fully to God out of who He created and redeemed you to be. It is not about God fixing or changing someone or something else in your life. It is about embracing what Jesus made available on the cross for you personally. A relationship with the living God will change you, and as you change the ways in which you respond, the world around you will change. It's about taking the log out of your own eye. When I actually trust in the salvation and freedom that Jesus bought on the cross for me, I begin to realize how, through His sacrifice, I can become a child of God. It is in the relationship of being a dependent child of God that I will know real freedom. When I begin to fully respond to God in the way He created me to be as His beloved child, I can begin to live as who God created me to be.

THE FREEDOM AND GRACE OF THE CROSS

Every single thing that keeps you in bondage—fear, anxiety, worry—is connected to the fact that you are not free in your own mind to be the son or daughter God calls you to be. It means there is something hampering your relationship with God that keeps you from fully trusting Him—trusting Him to not only make you free but to keep you free and take care of every single detail in your life. Proverbs 3:5-6 declares, "Trust in the Lord with all of your heart. Lean not on your understanding. In all your ways, in every detail, acknowledge Him, and He shall direct your path." There is no "maybe" here. God *shall* direct your path *if* you will trust Him in every single detail.

The greatest need of the human heart is to know who you really are and whose you really are. These needs are found and met in the cross of Jesus Christ where there is freedom and grace. Grace is not something that just gets you saved. The late James Ryle, a pastor from the Boulder Colorado Vineyard

Church who worked with Promise Keepers, has this definition of grace: "Grace is the empowering presence of God that enables me to be who God created me to be and to do all God created me to do."[2] It is not about my works or me trying to get myself free. It is about the empowering presence of God the Father who gives me the grace to be who I really am in Jesus' name. Freedom and grace go hand in hand. You cannot know true freedom without understanding that your freedom is tied into your identity as a son or daughter of a loving Father God.

If you're not living in freedom, you are in bondage. Jesus tried to explain this to the Jews. In John 8:31-32 Jesus is speaking to Jews who believe in Him, not to unbelieving Jews. How many know that it is possible for believers in Jesus to be deceived? If you don't think it's possible, read these verses again: *"To the Jews who had believed him, Jesus said, 'If you hold to my teaching, you are really my disciples. Then you will know the truth, and the truth will set you free'"* (John 8:31-32). The people listening replied, *"We are Abraham's descendants and have never been slaves of anyone. How can you say that we shall be set free?"* (John 8:33).

God has such a sense of humor! Here are the Jews telling Jesus they have never been slaves to anyone when their entire history is one of being enslaved in one way or another. Starting in Exodus 3, God calls a man at a burning bush to set His people free from slavery and bondage. Fast-forward and God has taken His people to the promised land and given them the blessing of the covenant. They plant themselves in the promised land, get comfortable and slippery with what they're doing, and don't hold to the covenant. The entire book of Judges is about Israel worshiping God, falling back into sin, being delivered by God, and then falling into sin all over again. They are constantly falling captive to sin that enslaves them.

Right when these Jews in John 8:33 are responding to Jesus that they have never been enslaved, they are actually living in bondage to the Roman empire. In verse 34, Jesus answered them, *"Very truly I tell you, everyone who sins is a slave to sin. Now a slave has no permanent place in the family, but a son belongs to it forever. So if the Son sets you free, you will be free indeed"* (John 8:34-36). He goes on to tell them that they have been listening to the father of lies, then He calls "the father of lies" their father.

BONDAGE TO BAD DEFINITIONS

Bondage can begin with bad definitions. There are definitions about God, our self, our world, and what is possible for us that actually can keep us in bondage and bring us to a place where we really don't have an understanding of what the target is. If your definition of freedom is wrong, you're going to be pushing toward something that will never bring you freedom while actually moving into more bondage.

Sometimes we define freedom by what we're not doing. We say, "I don't drink, smoke, or curse" and then look down on others who do those things. This can lead to what some call the gospel of sin management, which is about behavioral change and making sure that we are all just good boys and girls. In the gospel of sin management, we measure ourselves by ourselves and compare ourselves with ourselves to assure ourselves that we are behaving well.

If you look at First Corinthians 8, there is a word for that, and it is "stupid." Jesus didn't come to die so that you would have better behavior. He didn't come to die so that you would be a good boy or girl. When we limit the good news to that kind of definition, what we are actually limiting is our identity and what is possible for our life. We were created for more than we can possibly imagine. It's not a sin management issue; it's an identity issue. It is about walking by grace in the freedom of who you were really created by God to be.

John 8:36 says, *"So if the Son sets you free, you will be free indeed."* Those who receive the spirit of adoption as beloved sons and daughters of God, when it is extended to them through Jesus Christ, will live in true freedom from the bondage of sin and the lies of the devil. It really is just that simple.

In the name of Jesus, I speak liberty to you. I declare that you are no longer captive—you are free in Jesus' mighty name! The power of His blood sets you free and releases you from the prison of trauma. Thanks to Jesus, you can live in freedom of body, mind, and spirit.

NOTES

1. Bob Hamp, *Think Differently Live Differently: Keys to a Life of Freedom* (Think Differently Press, 2010).
2. Edith Adrian Matthies, *Walk with Me: A Life Lived with Joy* (Victoria, BC: Friesen Press, 2018), 193.

CHAPTER 8

The Journey to Freedom

I was a good Baptist boy. I walked the aisle at 13, was baptized, went to church every Sunday, and went to youth fellowship. I did everything I was supposed to do to please my parents, and I thought having God in my life was a good idea. I saw a lot of religion and heard a message of salvation preached every Sunday. Even though as Baptists we believed in eternal security, I felt like I needed to get saved all over again to make the preacher feel good. He was preaching a message of salvation every Sunday to a room full of people, many of whom had been church members for 40 years.

At the age of 19 I had a radical encounter with Jesus at a crisis point in my life and was saved. I had dropped out of school, a relationship had fallen apart, and I felt no purpose in my life. After this radical salvation encounter with Jesus, there was a change in my thinking and understanding and a softening in my heart toward God. In the next two years, I saw over 75 young people in a church of 150 people come to faith in Jesus Christ in our youth group. I then heard the call to go into ministry. I went to my denominational college and then on to seminary, and after graduation I began to pastor churches. I believed in God, trusted in Jesus, and read the Bible.

At this point in my walk with the Lord I was a cessationist who did not believe that what the Bible says was possible at the time it was written is still possible today. Whenever a Pentecostal or charismatic would come into my orbit, I would give that person a hard time, arguing with them and telling them they were crazy to believe miracles, signs, and wonders were for today.

Eventually I graduated with my Master of Divinity. I was finally a master of the divine. I went to pastor my first church in southern Illinois, ready and eager for a full-time pastoral position. The old bell that used to hang in the church belfry was in my front yard at the parsonage. Kids would come by and ring it at 3 A.M. Full of youthful vigor and the divine, I put everything I had learned in the past seven years—everything I had paid thousands of dollars to learn—to work in the church. After six months of pastoring, it seemed that everything that I had learned, all of the "amazing" church programs that I sought to implement to enable the church to grow...wasn't working. I had come to the end of myself and felt like a complete failure A mere six months later I was crying out to God. It's funny to me now, but it wasn't then. I had a lot of things going on. We were newly married, just over a year. Although Roxanne and I had a really good relationship, there was stuff going on with us. We had bondage in our lives; we had things that didn't seem to be right.

At that time there was a new network called Trinity Broadcasting Network (TBN). When we visited the church to candidate for the position of senior pastor in southern Illinois, we were in a hotel room and turned on the TV to see the news, and there on the screen was an evangelist. Now, at that time in my life I was not very kindly disposed toward TV evangelists. During my time in seminary, a bunch of us would sit on Sunday nights and watch TV evangelists and make fun of them. There was a guy called Reverend Ike. One of his disciples had a wall behind him of $100 bills as he preached a prosperity gospel. My seminary buddies and I had great fun making fun of Reverend Ike and many other TV evangelists.

That night in the hotel room in southern Illinois a guy came on the TV—an angry preacher who was sweating and screaming. I turned to Roxanne and said, "Look at this guy." We had a good laugh and then turned off the TV. Fast-forward a year later and I'm pretty depressed because nothing I am doing as a pastor is working. The people in our church love me, but things aren't working. Late one night I turned on the TV and there was the guy from TBN broadcasting live from Redding, California. His name was James Robison. I thought I'd just sit and have a few laughs.

Robison began to share about how as a leading evangelist he had walked with God and stood before millions of people and seen thousands come to faith in Jesus Christ, yet he had brokenness in his life. He never knew his dad, he had identity problems, he struggled with bondages in his life like lust, gluttony, and spirits of suicide. He spoke of how as he was standing ready to go in front of ten thousand people he would hear voices saying he should kill himself. I listened to him because I knew what that felt like. I knew what it was to have bondage in my life, some of which I thought would be taken care of because I got married. I can remember as a little child—I was an only child—being in my room at night and hearing voices in my head all the time and seeing monsters in my room. I'm not talking about just pretending to see them, but actually seeing them. I was always so afraid to go to sleep. The only way I could deal with the fear was to get my mind off of it with some sort of distraction. The habit of distraction to deal with fear carried over into my adulthood in the form of bondages.

So here I am as an adult watching James Robison's testimony and God is speaking to me. I ended up watching three of the four days of that crusade. The gist of it was a message of freedom. I realized that I was on a trajectory that wouldn't make it in ministry. When Robison mentioned a seminar in Dallas-Fort Worth led by a carpet cleaner named Milton Green, I heard the Holy Spirit say it was for me so I drove down by myself and went to the seminar.

I sat for three days under a carpet cleaner who did nothing but simply read the Word of God to us. God's Word opened my eyes to the spiritual warfare that is against every believer in Christ—that the devil is out to steal, kill, and destroy. Most of the scripture Green used came from the Old Testament. I came away from that seminar with a new understanding of just how deeply I was in bondage.

GENERATIONAL ROOTS OF BONDAGE

How many of you know that bondages often have a generational root? My great-grandfather was in the Freemasons, and there is a generational curse attached to Freemasonry that had come down the generational line to me. I had lust, fear, pride, anxiety, and believed the lie that all of this was part of my personality, was just who I was. I would ask God to forgive me of my sin and then repeat that sin over and over. It was a vicious cycle in my life. I was living from bad definitions. Here I was a life-long churchgoer, a "good boy," and I was living in bondage. Believers are not going to bring freedom to the world until the church gets free. We are not going to see harvest in America like other countries because the church in America isn't free, but that freedom is coming.

I went back home from that seminar a free man. I had 14 hours on the road and praised Jesus the whole way. When I got home, my wife had a new man on her hands, a wild man. I was reading the Bible, listening to tapes, and praying as I experienced that glorious moment in time when all of a sudden you know God has so touched you and set you free that you get crazy for God and it is okay to be crazy.

Then Halloween came. Halloween was one of our favorite holidays. We had all sorts of Halloween decorations. Roxanne loved to decorate for Halloween and so she proceeded to put up all of her decorations. She had a large ceramic witch on a broomstick on a pumpkin. In my "on fire for God" state, I was taken aback and said we couldn't have any of that in our house because it was from the devil. I was right, but I said it in the wrong way.

My problem was that although I had been set free from demons, I started seeing them behind every bush because my focus wasn't on Jesus. My focus was on what was wrong. From that skewed vantage point everybody was wrong except me. Even though I had been set free from a bondage of pride, guess what the devil was doing? There I stood in the doorway of our parsonage arguing with Roxanne about Halloween decorations. At one point I had enough. Thinking that I had a spirit of wisdom on me, I said, "In the name of Jesus, you demon, stop talking and come out of my wife." How many of you know that was a spirit of stupid!

Roxanne is a woman of integrity, honesty, and great love. She looked me in the eye and said, "Mike, this ain't no demon talking to you, this is your wife." Needless to say, I repented. We worked it out and everything was fine. In fact, because God works everything for the good of those who love Him and are called according to His purpose (see Rom. 8:28), what came out as a result of that moment of stupidity is that Roxanne got set free from some bondage she had carried for generations. The bottom line was we got set free as a family from generational curses and bondages. We had been experiencing difficulty having children, and the doctors weren't sure we could ever have children. Thanks to the freedom we received, we conceived a child very soon afterward.

You can be in bondage to bad definitions of freedom. You can be in bondage from misunderstanding your true identity. If you can get your definition of Papa God right, then you will get your definition about who you are right. Once you get it straight in your head that God is a loving Father, your other definitions will get straight as well. Pastor Bill Johnson preaches that anything you think about God that you don't see in Jesus, you need to get rid of.

STEPPING INTO YOUR TRUE IDENTITY

Every single label you've listened to about yourself, every lie said about you, is absolutely about stealing, killing, and destroying the dream of God for your life. As long as you believe that stuff, you will never enter into the fullness of who you were created to be. You were created for more than you could ever imagine. The greatest tool the enemy uses is to get us in a place where we doubt who we really are. The apostle Paul, when writing letters to the churches, always starts the letter, "To the saints of...." By *saints* he means "holy ones." All of these churches were struggling. They were a mess, yet Paul didn't see that as their identity. He saw them as God intended them to be and called them up to that better place.

It is not about your behavior at this moment; it is about who God calls you to be, and He is calling you right now to step into your true identity. *"Therefore, if anyone is in Christ, the new creation has come: The old has gone, the new is here!"* (2 Cor. 5:17). This includes your history. In Romans 6, the "old man," your old self, is buried with Christ and raised with Christ into new life. We become new in Christ. Not only do I now understand who God is, I also have a new definition of who I am. I no longer have to be in bondage to my history. How many of you know that you can be in bondage even after you come to Christ, just as I was?

All of us need to deal with our family history because what came before us is not necessarily what God intends. It is an awesome thing if you know you have a great, healthy family history; however, many will find things in their family tree that need correction by the hand of God. There was a time when the Hutchings side of my family tree was a mystery to me. One day after my mom and dad had passed on to glory, I decided to search my family tree using Ancestry.com. By looking at death certificates, I saw that my dad's father died of alcoholism in an institution in 1933. My dad had never talked about his dad. There were 12 children in the family, and only my grandfather had children. My grandfather died of alcoholism, three of his sisters died in an institution in Kentucky from conditions leading to insanity, and two others died of suicide.

The more I looked at my family tree, the more I understood what had been going on in my own life, why I had been hearing voices and seeing demons as a young child. Before I came fully to Christ, I was an angry and mean drunk. In high school we could go out and buy booze. The first time I had hard liquor, I was camping with friends and I tore up the entire camp in a rage that was alcohol induced. I don't remember a thing. I just remember being arrested. Every time I drank alcohol there was a buzz in my head that started doing something to me that no one wanted to be around. There was a generational curse on me of insanity and alcoholism that had passed through my family. Everyone would tell me that even though I was a believer, I would have to live under that curse and be ashamed. I want to be clear right now that I am no longer defined by my history, my family's history, or anything else the devil has tried to steal from my life. I am no longer living under the curse from my family line, no longer in bondage. I have repented and prayed over myself, my wife, and my children and grandchildren, thanking Jesus for showing me His truths and setting me free. The ministry God has given to me in PTSD is a direct vengeance against the enemy for what he stole from my family's life, in Jesus' name.

FREEDOM IS A JOURNEY, NOT A DESTINATION

Many of you reading this are struggling with weaknesses, habits, and bondages that are causing you to feel guilty or ashamed. I want you to know that there is freedom for you if you will allow Jesus Christ to come and set you free in a way that you could never do for yourself. And not only is there freedom for you, but Jesus will take your greatest struggles, your greatest weaknesses and addictions and turn them into a platform for your greatest ministry. Jesus is not about condemnation; He is about restoration.

Isaiah 61 tells of the Day of Jubilee, when that which was stolen from us or taken through our own choices is completely restored. The restoration of Jesus over your life is your Day of Jubilee, the day you realize you have been walking under oppression, the day when the chains of bondage are broken off you and you are set free through the love of God and the price He paid in Jesus Christ. On that day, God will give you a mantle of praise instead of a spirit of heaviness. The spirit of heaviness is the history, guilt, and shame we carry when we don't understand what is possible in Jesus. God intends that we live as a people of no more guilt, no more shame, no more condemnation, walking free as children of a loving Father, in Jesus' mighty name.

There is no way I would ever be at Global Awakening in my current position had I not allowed God to take me through those seasons of letting Him deal with my soul, understanding the bondage, and then walking in freedom. Before I got set free, I had a spirit of lying because I had been trained by parents who said I had to please everyone. When you try to make everyone happy, you make no one happy. You have to lie, tell stories, and hate yourself because you know exactly what you're doing. When I got set free, I confessed and repented, and half of my church left. The ones who stayed loved me, applauded me, and helped me build that church as an amazing work of God. It was no longer based on a foundation of lies, but on the truth of God. I had to stand in front of my church and my family and confess things I had never confessed in my life.

Often we get free of some bondages and realize there are deeper things, other bondages that are enslaving us. If this is you, don't feel condemned. More often than not, God doesn't clean us up all at once. Freedom is not a destination; it is a journey. We live in a place of walking with Jesus, allowing Him to show us those things that are keeping us from the fullness of our identity. Daily He renews our mind. The only thing we can give God besides our praise is our brokenness—that which holds us back from being fully identified in Him. Freedom is available right now in Jesus' name.

CHAPTER 9

ACTIVATION: RECEIVE YOUR HEALING

I f you have read this far in the book, I want you to know that your healing is at hand. Right now, God is inviting you on the journey from captivity to freedom. I believe this is a journey that you have wanted to take for a very long time, but you have not known how. Many of you have been so traumatized that you are afraid to take the journey to healing. In the name of Jesus, I want you to know Holy Spirit is here right now as your comforter, your friend, the one who knows everything you have been through. He is not here to expose you, further traumatize you, or hurt you in any way. God is here to heal you and take the shattered pieces of your broken heart and put them back together again. He is here to restore you and give you a life of freedom and purpose that you can walk out in peace all the days of your life. He is eager to cast off the false identity you have been struggling under and reveal your true God-given identity to you because God has plans for you:

> *"For I know the plans I have for you," declares the Lord, "plans to prosper you and not to harm you, plans to give you hope and a future"* (Jeremiah 29:11).

GOD'S INVITATION

God is inviting you into a safe place right now even though it may not feel safe at times because of things that will try and trigger you. Be assured that God is with you and that He has defeated the enemy of your soul on the cross of His Son, Jesus Christ. The enemy has no power to undo the cross. Jesus has all authority as it has been given to Him by God the Father. Any trigger you may feel is the feeble attempt of a defeated foe to maintain control over your life.

Right now, by the power of the blood of Jesus, I welcome Holy Spirit to come upon you as your comforter, helper, healer, and deliverer. I declare the forgiveness of God in Jesus' name. No matter what you have done or what has been done to you, you are free and no longer defined by your history. You are now defined by who your God calls you to be, which is His beloved child.

By the power of the blood of Jesus, I break the power of shame you carry due to the trauma or traumas you have experienced. What was done to you or what you have experienced does not speak to who you are. You no longer carry shame because none of God's children have shame.

I break the power of guilt that you carry for sin or things you did to cope with your pain. In the name of Jesus, there is no condemnation. The law of the spirit of life has set you free from the law of sin and death.

By the power of the declaration of Isaiah 61, I declare the spirit of the Lord God is here to bring good news to your broken heart. He is here to heal you and declare liberty and freedom. Right now, He is bringing comfort for mourning, joy for sorrow, a mantle of praise for the spirit of heaviness through divine exchange.

I sever every single assignment of the evil one against you. In the name of Jesus, I command spirits of trauma, torment, and fear to leave now in the name of Jesus. I sever your assignment against this person by the power of the blood of Jesus Christ.

Spirit of suicide, I break your power, and I command you to stop speaking right now. I speak to murder and rage, and I sever your assignment. In the name of Jesus, you no longer have a place in the life of the person reading this. I sever right now the spirit of death. I say to you, reader, that you carry the same spirit that raised Jesus' dead body from the grave. I command the spirit of death to leave you now in Jesus' name.

I cancel and break off depression, oppression, insanity, mental illness, and the spirit of bipolar or multiple personality disorder in Jesus' name. I sever your assignment from the person reading this in Jesus' name.

I sever right now the spirit of lust, of perversion, of sexual violation and slavery off the one reading this in Jesus' name. I declare that chains and shackles of sexual perversion and lust are broken off of you in Jesus' name. You are no longer, in any way, shape, or form, under the thumb of sexual perversion. I break the power of pornography. I sever the hold it has upon your soul and mind. I command the images and memories of pornography to dry up and die right now.

I invite you to put your hand on your heart as I speak healing to your broken heart in Jesus' name. Let the power of Holy Spirit come now to pick up pieces and put them back together so you can walk in the freedom of being God's child and in His grace to be everything you were created to be and do. I declare that as healing comes to your heart, the shalom of God that brings wholeness and wellness will affect your mind, will, and emotions, and also your body, in the name of Jesus.

I invite you to put your right hand on your head. In the name of Jesus, I speak to every traumatic image and memory in the right lobe of your brain and command these images to dry up and die. I sever the neuropathway that leads to these traumatic images and memories. I sever your seeing, smelling, tasting, touching, and hearing from being triggered through these neuropathways. I sever every lie and stronghold connected with traumatic images and memories. I pray for fresh faith and the truth of the word of God to replace those lies and images and memories. I command the memory center to wake up, wake up, wake up! Let there be a free flow of memory from the memory center so that what is restored to you are good memories about your life. Your mind is no longer held hijacked by traumatic images and memories.

I speak healing to any concussions, traumatic brain injuries, or anything that has caused your brain to not operate in the way it was originally intended by God. I command rewiring of the brain and proper neuron function, in the name of Jesus. I break the diagnosis of ADHD, dyslexia, loss of cognitive function, in the name of Jesus. I pray healing over auditory and visual processing, in the name of Jesus.

I command any masking of a trauma that looks like mental illness that was really caused by trauma to be healed, in the name of Jesus. I declare healthy functions and connections be restored between the right and left lobe of your brain. I declare the right lobe be completely restored and healed right now by the power of the blood of Jesus Christ. Thank You, Father.

> I speak healing to all systems of your body and their functions, in the mighty name of Jesus.

I speak to your nervous system that includes your eyes and ears, your brain and spinal cord, and your nerves, and command it to be healed. All chronic nerve pain must leave now in the name of Jesus.

I command the endocrine system consisting of your network of glands that release and regulate your hormones be set back to its original settings so that all glands operate properly with the right flow of hormones, in the name of Jesus.

I speak to your musculoskeletal system consisting of your muscles, bones, cartilage, and ligaments and declare every memory from a traumatic event be released now from muscles and other areas so that all pain associated with accidents and ungodly touch between humans is removed and replaced by the peace and shalom of God.

I speak healing to your circulatory system consisting of your heart, blood vessels, and lymphatic system and declare healing in Jesus' name.

I speak healing to your urinary tract system consisting of your kidneys, bladder, and related ducts, and declare them healed and restored in the name of Jesus.

I speak healing to all aspects of your digestive system consisting of your mouth, esophagus, stomach, and bowels, and declare it healed so that you are able to eat of the healthy foods on God's earth as He intends and digest them well so that they nourish and sustain your body all the days of your life.

I speak to your reproductive system in the name of Jesus, declaring healing and proper functioning so that within the bonds of holy marriage you may be fruitful and multiply as God intends.

I speak to your integumentary system and declare that your skin, hair, nails, and oil and sweat glands will function as God intends to protect your body and help regulate temperature and the elimination of waste from your body. I declare all aspects of this system of your body that have been compromised to be healed, in Jesus' name.

I speak to your respiratory system consisting of your nose, upper airways, and lungs, and declare it off-limits to the enemy. I declare that the breath of life God has put within you to sustain you will not be compromised in any way, and any and all damage to your respiratory system is healed, in the name of Jesus.

I speak to your immune system and command it come into alignment with God's will for your body, to act as your physical defense system against all harmful organisms all the days of your life.

I speak to your sleep and say according to Proverbs 3:24 you shall no longer lie down in fear, that it is your Father's pleasure to give His beloved children sweet sleep. I command a resetting of the sleep center in your brain to experience six to eight hours of uninterrupted sleep every night. I command all nightmares to go, all night tremors to go, night sweats to go, in Jesus' name. I invite God's holy angels to come around your bed in your bedroom so that your bed is a place of rest and peace, not warfare, in the name of Jesus.

By the power of the blood of Jesus Christ, I declare you are no longer defined by your history; you are defined by who your God calls you to be. I declare that you are a new creation in Christ. The old has passed away; all things have become new in your life.

NEW CREATION DECLARATION BLESSING

I invite you now to make the following new creation declaration over your life.

> *This is who my Father says I am: I am a child of the King. I am a co-heir with Jesus. All Jesus bought and paid for is my inheritance. I am loved. I am forgiven. I am cleaned by the blood. I am accepted in the Beloved. I am filled with His Spirit. I have angels protecting me and assisting me in the ministry of Jesus. I am united with Jesus. I have been*

crucified with Christ. I died with Him. I was buried with Him. I was raised with Him. I am seated with Him in the heavenlies far above all rule, all power, all authority, and above every name that is named, not only in this age, but also in the one to come. Therefore, I carry the authority of Christ. I have authority over sickness, over sin, over demons, and over the world. I am the salt of the earth. I am the light of the world. All things work together for my good because I love God, and I am called according to His purpose, which is for me to be conformed to the image and likeness of Christ. I can do all things through Christ, because greater is He who is in me than he who is in the world.

CONCLUSION

God intends that we live "unbroken," with an understanding of our God-given identity—who He created us to be. Because we are all born into and live in a sinful world, most of us are living with a broken version of our true self. The enemy of our souls, the devil, wants us to live as brokenhearted captives. God, our loving heavenly Father, sent His Son Jesus Christ to live on earth and die on the cross to set us free from the devil's bondage, to bind up our broken hearts and make us whole again. It is only through Jesus Christ that we become healed and whole.

In Christ, you are a new creation. The old has passed away; all things have become new. You are loved, you are accepted, you are forgiven, and you are adopted into God's family. You are a co-heir with Jesus, which means that His inheritance from God is also your inheritance. Jesus lived an unbroken life and that unbrokenness is available to you.

God has a purpose and a destiny for your life. He has plans for you that are to be carried out before your feet leave this earth. You are called by God according to His purpose for your life. You have a destination and that destination is heaven. Until you get there, you have an assignment on this earth, which is to help bring heaven to the earth by being like Jesus to the world around you.

Your life is a connection between heaven and earth. When you are struggling with brokenness, that connection gets a lot of static on the line—so much static sometimes that you can't hear the voice of Father God; you can't hear or feel His unconditional love for you. When you invite Jesus into your life to heal your brokenness, He repairs your connection to the heart of the Father so that God's love can freely flow to you once again as it did when He created you in your mother's womb. The Holy Spirit is like your internet connection to the Father, and the Spirit has unlimited bandwidth. And guess what? It's free! Jesus already paid the price for your restoration to God. You can have a lifetime of free connection to the Father through Jesus. I think that's a good deal. I think that is the best deal you will ever find anywhere.

God has a covenant blessing for you. What does that mean? God's covenant blessing is a commitment He initiated between Himself and humankind so that we might live in relationship with Him where we can experience wholeness, lacking nothing. That covenant blessing is available to you through Jesus Christ. Thanks to the power of God's grace—His gift of goodwill given to you—nothing you have done or had done to you can disqualify you from receiving God's covenant blessing.

Mental trauma is an injury to the soul of a person. No action by another person can heal an injury to your soul. Therapy and medication can help, but only God can take the broken pieces of your mind, will, and emotions and put them back together. The devil has a "no hope" message that says your brokenness is forever, that you are going to live hopeless and helpless for the rest of your life. That is a lie! God's message is one of hope—hope in His resurrection power that raised Jesus from the dead to overcome every scheme of the devil over your life.

You may be saying to yourself right now, "Well, Mike, all this Jesus stuff is well and good, but I don't want to go there. I just want you to say some nice words over me and have all this torment stop." I'm here to tell you that it is only through Jesus that wholeness and healing will come to you. There is a holistic healing that only Jesus brings to our shattered souls. He alone is able to reintegrate the pieces of our mind, will, and emotions. Your destiny and purpose in this life is to glorify God with the shalom of God upon you.

My friend Lynn Eldridge understands what it is to live in wholeness with God's shalom upon her to the glory of God. Like many of us, Lynn was born into a dysfunctional family with ungodly generational roots that brought iniquity and personal sin. Here is her testimony.

> I was raised in a Pentecostal church. Throughout my life I struggled with undiagnosed mental illness in my family that triggered in me spirits of rebellion, rage, addiction, and bulimia. Both my parents had either obsessive-compulsive disorder, schizophrenia, bipolar disorder, anorexia, bulimia, and addictions, but were considered successful by the standards of the world. I left my

Pentecostal church because I was angry at God. I had tried to live for Him, but because of lack of teaching on scripture I was perishing and so was my family (see Hosea 4:6).

At age 35 I was diagnosed as bipolar with borderline personality disorder at Hanley-Hazelden drug and alcohol treatment center. I was on every imaginable psychotropic drug cocktail that doctors could concoct to try to bring me some relief from the torment I had been experiencing for the past seventeen years. I had acupuncture; I was in therapy sometimes three days a week.

Winters were worse because of the deep depressions. I was into New Age, Buddhism, Hinduism, you name it. I attended AA and was sober for six years but continued struggling with the torment until I decided to medicate it myself again by going back to addiction. In March/April of 2011, I admitted myself to the Menninger Clinic at Baylor University in Houston, Texas because I was told it was the best in the nation. I had reached such a level of torment and emotional pain that I was suicidal. I thought Menninger was my last hope for relief. After weeks of testing there was some talk of keeping me some place that was "more secure." I did not want to be committed because then I knew I would be unable kill myself. I somehow was allowed to check myself out and went home more hopeless and extremely afraid of being committed.

My cousin invited me to go see a "healer" at a local church in June or July of 2011. I ended up going to a local Healing Room[1] where I had an encounter with Jesus—I just felt the power of His presence. I learned about generational curses and received what I now know were deliverance prayers every week. I was confessing, repenting, forgiving, and renouncing generational iniquity and personal sin. In approximately two months, by the end of November 2011, I was off of *all* medications and living my life without torment and experiencing significant peace, hope, and joy! Now, over six years later, I am still pursuing Jesus with all that I am and all that I

have as I live in His peace. Jesus is the
only Way; there was no other way.

God has already made a decision about you. He
has already chosen to love you with an everlasting love that will never fail, and a commitment to
see you become the very best of the dream He had
for you before you were born. All of the sin, all the
addictions and lies over your life have already been
dealt with by God through Jesus on the cross. God
has made His decision about you; He has decided in
your favor. All you have to do is step into the truth of
what God says about you. There was a time when I
had difficulty experiencing God's love for me. I had
difficulty understanding the truth about God's love
and His healing that is available to me. I had obstacles in my mind that were causing me to struggle. I
was full of shame and guilt. I was a pastor standing in
front of my congregation every week and preaching
about God's love and feeling like the worst hypocrite
because I wasn't experiencing God's love. Then God
invited me into the dream He had for my life and I
received it!

By its very nature, an invitation is something
that is to be received. God is inviting you to enter
into the dream He has for your life. It begins by
embracing the truth that you are the righteousness

of God through Jesus Christ. It begins by receiving the spirit of adoption He is extending to you.

> *For those who are led by the Spirit of God are the children of God. The Spirit you received does not make you slaves, so that you live in fear again; rather, the Spirit you received brought about your adoption to sonship. And by him we cry, "Abba, Father"* (Romans 8:14-15).

Your heavenly Father wants to give you His godly boundaries to live within so that you can receive all of His blessings for your life. He wants to go to the roots of your broken places and pull out your brokenness by the roots so that you don't have to live with it anymore. He wants you to live free from the bondages of fear, anxiety, and worry. God is not offering you sin management; He is offering you freedom. Remember, freedom is not a destination; it is a journey. God promises to walk the journey with you every day of your life so that you can live free. Your healing is at hand, every day. God's mercy and grace are new every morning.

Greater is he who is in you than he who is in the world. You are seated with Christ in heavenly places. Everything is under the feet of Jesus. Therefore, everything is under your feet when you receive Him as your Lord and Savior. You have not been given a spirit of fear but of power, love, and a sound mind. You have a sound mind because you have the mind of Christ. You think God's thoughts. God speaks to you, and you are led by Him. There is nothing in all of this earth that can stand against you if God is for you, and He is for you. All things work together for your good because you love God and are called according to His purpose. His purpose for you is to look more and more like Jesus every day. You look more like Jesus today than you did yesterday. You will look more like Jesus tomorrow than you do today. You have a destination. You are going to heaven. In the meantime, you have an assignment to bring heaven to earth. Your life is a temple for the Holy Spirit, a connection between heaven and earth. Everywhere you go, the kingdom of God goes. Everywhere you go, the love of God goes. Everywhere you go, the glory of God goes. Angels are with you. You are more than a conqueror because God loves you. You are free, in the name of Jesus!

NOTE

1. Cal Pierce, "Birth of Healing Rooms," Healing Rooms Ministries, https://healingrooms.com/index.php?page_id=2569.

Prayer Model for Deliverance from Trauma

This prayer model for healing from post-traumatic stress disorder is Holy Spirit-led. It is about listening to Holy Spirit and following what He tells you, the prayer minister, to do. Sometimes Holy Spirit will tell you to go through all the steps in this model because that is what the person needs. Sometimes He will tell you to skip a step or two. Only the Holy Spirit knows what the person you are ministering to needs. You must learn to listen and follow His lead in order for the person to be healed. Trust that you will have the ability to hear and do not be hard on yourself if you don't get it right every time. There is grace in God's presence. He is in charge. Ministering to others is a learning process; it is about learning that God is the healer and He desires to work through you to heal others.

With that being said, I have seen people who have no idea how to minister healing from PTSD simply read aloud through the steps of this prayer model and people are healed. It is not about a model or a method. It is about God as the Healer. Models and methods give us a framework, a place to begin, and what happens after that is up to God.

Step 1: Interview

ASK: *What was the traumatic event in your life? You don't need to give details, just state briefly what the event was.* (Example: car accident, child abuse, parental abuse, witnessed a violent event, etc.) If they are a military active duty or veteran, say: *Thank you for your service to our country. Thank you for laying down your life so that we can be free. Your service was not in vain because we are still free. Welcome home!*

Keep eye contact during prayer time.

Step 2: Explain what you will do and receive permission

ASK: *I will be taking authority in Jesus' name and commanding out all the effects that the traumatic event(s) you mentioned have had over your being. Do I have your permission to do so? Do I have permission to lay my hand on your shoulder or hold your hand as I pray for you?*

Do not raise your voice to bring healing. Keep a calm, even voice. Express love, peace, joy, and faith.

Step 3: Forgive

> **PRAY:** *If there's anything you feel you have done wrong as a result of the trauma that was done to you, take a few minutes to get quiet with God and confess to Him. You don't need to tell me about it; just close your eyes for this part, talk directly to God, and ask Him to forgive you. While you are praying about this, allow the blood of Jesus Christ to cleanse you of sin. This is for anything that comes up in your memory about anything you've done as a result of the trauma. Know that the forgiveness of God is already here. All you have to do is receive it.*

> *Thank You, Jesus, for Your blood that cleanses us from all unrighteousness.*

After a few minutes, move on. (They are not confessing to you.)

ASK: *Everything I do from here on is part of the benefit of Jesus Christ dying on the cross and rising from the grave. If you haven't received Jesus Christ, this would be a great time to do it. Would you like to do that?*

If YES, lead them into a prayer of receiving Jesus Christ and the power of forgiveness of sins through His blood and go to Step 4.

If NO, then pray a blessing over them and pray for God's healing and restoration. Extend the love of God and the grace of God to them, then end the prayer session.

Step 4: Declare Isaiah 61:1-3

> **PRAY:** *Holy Spirit, we welcome Your presence over _____ to fulfill the mission of Jesus according to Isaiah 61:1-3, which says that God sent Jesus to bind up the brokenhearted, to proclaim freedom for captives, and to release prisoners from darkness. Jesus wants to give you a crown of beauty instead of ashes,*

the oil of joy instead of mourning, and a garment of praise instead of a spirit of despair.

Step 5: Break off Shame (keep eye contact with the person)

PRAY: *Now I'm going to break off all feelings of shame, guilt, condemnation, and responsibility for anything you have done, been ordered to do, or that was done to you. In the name of Jesus Christ of Nazareth, by the power of His blood, all **shame** is broken off of your life in Jesus' name. You are no longer defined by your history, by your experience of others, by your experience of yourself, or by any traumatic event or recurring pattern that has happened in your life. I break shame off of you in the name of Jesus Christ of Nazareth.*

PRAY: *No matter what you have done, if you've asked the Father to release you of that sin, forgiveness is yours in Jesus' name. So by the power of Jesus' blood, I break off all **guilt and condemnation** for anything you have done and anything you have witnessed. And I declare*

*that there is therefore now no condem-
nation for those who are in Christ Jesus
(Romans 8:1). You are a new creation
in Christ.*

PRAY: *By the power of the blood of Jesus
Christ, I declare over you that you are not
responsible for the abuse/harm that you
suffered. You are not responsible for that
which injured your body and your soul.
In the name of Jesus Christ of Nazareth,
I cleanse you from that in Jesus' name.
I break off the power of* **responsibility** *for those acts. I declare that you are
no longer defined by your history. What
people have done to you does not declare
who you are, in Jesus' name.*

Step 6: Healing Soul Wounds

Soul wounds caused by traumatic experiences
and/or actions become doorways for evil spirits
to torment. *Be led by Holy Spirit; listen for words
of knowledge* as you declare physical healing over
any wound or injury associated with trauma. (See
"Spirits of..." on next page.)

PRAY: *By the blood of Jesus, I call
down healing to your heart. I bind up
your broken heart that you've carried*

for years. In the name of Jesus Christ of Nazareth, I break the power of fear and anxiety over your life, and I speak healing to the wounds of fear and anxiety. I break the power of trauma over your life, and I speak healing to the wounds of trauma in Jesus' name.

For those who have been sexually violated at any time in their life:

PRAY: *In the name of Jesus Christ, I sever every soul tie that was created between you and the person who violated and abused you. I cancel that assignment and every work of darkness that was on that person that has been attacking you, and in Jesus' name we close every door of access and declare that you are free from the influence of every power of darkness, particularly lust, perversion, and control, in Jesus' name.*

I break the power of abuse (sexual, physical, verbal) over your life, and I speak healing to the wounds of abuse in Jesus' name. I break the power of _____ over your life, and I speak healing to the wounds of _____ in Jesus' name. (Fill in applicable issues from the list below.)

Spirits of: *trauma, torment, broken-heartedness, depression, bitterness, despair, rejection, unforgiveness, hopelessness, abandonment, suicide, horror, loneliness, unworthiness, grief, fear of being alone, manipulation, death, fear of being abused again, rage, murder, revenge, divorce/disunity, disunity from Jesus, mental illness, dementia, and any other afflicting spirits, fear of _____.*

Lies that are believed such as: *"God is not going to protect me. God is punishing me. I will have to live with this for the rest of my life."*

PRAY: *In Jesus' name, I command all afflicting and tormenting spirits I've mentioned above to leave you and never return. And to all of the associated cosmic spirits, I say, "The Lord rebuke you!" In Jesus' name, I cancel every assignment of the powers of darkness and all tormenting spirits against your spirit, mind, and body. I cancel all of the lies the enemy had you believe in* *the name of Jesus. And I cancel all pro-gramming from the lies of the enemy in the name of Jesus Christ of Nazareth. I pray healing to your mind, to any strong-holds or lies you've been believing, and I declare those lies and strongholds must come be destroyed in Jesus' name.*

PRAY: *I ask Holy Spirit to fill you with His holy living water to cleanse you from head to toe, healing all the wounds from all of these afflicting spirits. Holy Spirit, fill him/her to overflowing, and every area trauma has occupied, fill with Your love, peace, joy, grace, and power.*

Step 7: Protection

The person is protected when you close all path-ways and doors of access to tormenting spirits and declare the promise of protection according to Psalm 91.

Speak calmly and with authority in faith, trust, peace, and love.

PRAY: *In the name of Jesus Christ of Nazareth, I close all pathways, portals, or means of access or connections that allow tormenting spirits to bring fear, worry, anxiety, paranoia, nightmares,* *night terrors, insomnia, or traumatic images to you. And I declare Psalm 91 over you: The Lord is your refuge and your fortress. You can trust Him. He will save you from the fowler's snare and from the deadly pestilence. Under His wings you will find refuge; His faithfulness will be your shield and rampart. You will not fear the terror of night, nor the arrow that flies by day. A thousand may fall at your side, ten thousand at your right hand, but it will not come near you. For He will command His angels to guard you in all your ways.*

Step 8: Healing

In this step you will:

- Pray for healing for the mind and body systems that may have been affected by trauma.

- Disconnect the five senses from being triggers to the trauma.

- Ask Holy Spirit to reconnect the left and right brain.

- Declare freedom to the mind, body, and spirit.

PRAY: In the name of Jesus Christ of Nazareth, I speak to your body and I command healing to all the systems of your body including the skeletal system, lymphatic and immune system, muscular system, respiratory system, nervous system, digestive and excretory system, endocrine system, urinary and renal system, cardiovascular system, reproductive system, integumentary system (hair, skin, nails, and sweat glands).

By the authority of Jesus Christ and by the power of His blood, I cancel out any muscle memories, skin memories, and any memories in your brain that are associated with these traumatic events.

PRAY: In the name of Jesus Christ and by the power of His blood, I speak directly to each of your five senses and I disconnect them from being triggers to the traumatic events in your life.

- **Sight** (snap fingers)
- **Hearing** (snap fingers)
- **Tasting** (snap fingers)
- **Smelling** (snap fingers)
- **Feeling** (snap fingers)

I disconnect each of these five senses from
any images, ideas, or memories of the
traumatic events in _____'s life.

PRAY: *Holy Spirit, I ask You to reinte-*
grate all connections between the left
and right brain and that You restore
all healthy connections in the brain. I
declare healthy connections between
your spirit, soul, and body in Jesus'
name. Your past experiences and actions
no longer have a hold over you, and your
five senses are no longer triggers to trau-
matic events you've experienced.

Step 9: Release and Declare Freedom

Pray that the Lord release the person from
imprisonment or captivity associated with the expe-
riences/actions. Then pray for them to be released
from any vows or oaths they spoke as a result of
the trauma.

PRAY: *According to Isaiah 61:1-3, in*
Jesus' name I speak liberty to you. You
are no longer captive. You are set free
in Jesus' name from anything that was
done to you. In the name of Jesus, what-
ever you have done that was in any way,
shape, or form harmful to anyone as a

result of these traumatic experiences,
I declare that the power of the blood of
Christ has set you free. In Jesus' name,
I declare you are released from prison.
You are no longer in prison for what
was done to you or for what you have
done. The shackles and chains are off of
you. You are free in the name of Jesus!
I declare freedom to your spirit, mind,
and body.

Step 10: Identity in Christ

Declare the identity of the person as a royal son or daughter of a loving Father and speak a blessing. Declare God's blessings over them.

Look them in the eye, smile, and declare their identity as son or daughter. Memorize this!

PRAY: *Now you are going to declare*
your new identity in Christ by repeating
each line after me:
I am a new creation in Christ.
The old has passed away.
All things have become new.
I am in Jesus and Jesus is in me.
Greater is He who is in me than he who is
in the world.

I am loved and I am forgiven; I am washed by His blood (make sure they know what this means).

I am accepted by a loving Father who loves me no matter what.

In Jesus' name, I am seated with Christ in heavenly places.

I am His workmanship created to do good works for His glory.

I am more than a conqueror through Him who loves me.

I am no longer a victim (of any of the spirits mentioned or any traumatic events).

I am a victor; I am an overcomer in Jesus' name.

Everything in my life comes from the Father who is good; therefore, all things work together for my good because I love God and I'm called according to His purposes.

Because I believe in Jesus, I have an assignment.

I'm going to heaven, and in the meantime I have an assignment here.

I'm bringing heaven to earth.

I carry the power of God by Jesus in Holy Spirit.

The very same Spirit who raised Jesus from the dead lives in me.

Therefore, I have no fear.

God has not given me a spirit of fear but of power, and love, and a sound mind.

I carry perfect love.

Perfect love casts out all fear.

I am loved because my Father loves me.

I claim this new identity for myself in the name of Jesus Christ of Nazareth.

Final Words of Encouragement

EXPLAIN: *These prayers are not a magic wand that will suddenly make everything wonderful. This prayer model brings breakthrough so that now you can deal with life at a normal level of functioning rather than at a traumatized level. I encourage you to get plugged into a church community if you are not in one already. I encourage you to read scripture and memorize key verses that will help you keep your healing. The enemy will try to come back and steal your* *healing by lying to you about your healing. If you continue to stay in the church and stay in the Word of God as found in the Bible, you will become stronger and be victorious. I encourage you to go to a counselor or a healing room for additional prayer. I also encourage you to command any evil spirits or lies to leave you whenever you are feeling oppressed. **If** the feelings start to come back, you have authority in Jesus to tell them "**no**."*

__SPEAK:__ I speak peace, love, and abundant grace over you. I encourage you to obtain a Healing PTSD prayer card so that you may speak identity declarations over yourself every day.

APPENDIX B

VIETNAM VETERANS

There have numerous reports over the years of Vietnamese Buddhist priests declaring curses over American soldiers during the Vietnam War. The curses went something like this:

- They would be angry men and women all their lives.

- They would never find rest.

- They would have a wandering spirit.

When these soldiers returned to the United States, they were rejected and began to believe that they did not belong. They were not allowed to process their experience and isolated themselves, experiencing shame and guilt for their faithful service to our country.

PRAY

I thank you for your service to your country.

I ask forgiveness on behalf of the United States of America for failure to honor you and welcome you home when you returned from war.

I break off all belief in the lies spoken over you. I break off the lie that you do not belong, that you are rejected, and that you should carry guilt or shame for your service to your country.

I renounce and break agreement with the curses spoken over you.

BREAK THE CURSES

I bless you and break off of you a wandering spirit. I settle in you that you have a home, and I welcome you back to America. I speak "Shalom" into you.

*I break off of you the spirit of death.
I speak life into you. The Lord says,
"**Live!**"*

FORGIVENESS

*I invite you now to forgive those who
were your enemy in battle and to forgive
anyone in Vietnam or in the military
who hurt you.*

*I invite you to forgive the American gov-
ernment and anyone who hurt you.*

*I invite you to forgive those who offended
you or rejected you.*

Declare over them:

"Welcome home!"

APPENDIX C

TESTIMONIES OF GOD'S HEALING OF PTSD

VIDEO LINKS

- Miracle PTSD testimony feat. Dr. Randy Clark: https://www.youtube.com/watch?v=cCwffVgvSlE&feature=youtu.be

- Veteran healed of PTSD, TBI, insomnia, back and neck injuries: https://www.godhealsptsd .com/testimonies/2019/8/19/video -veteran-healed-of-ptsd-and-back-injury

- Woman healed of trauma by viewing healing PTSD video:

https://www.youtube.com/
watch?v=Lyb95kaLec8&feature=youtu.be

- Vietnam vet healed from PTSD:
  https://www.youtube.com/watch?v
  =oLErYYVXJhg&feature=youtu.be

- Army veteran healed of PTSD symptoms
  and sleep disorder: https://youtu.be/
  nPKecdj-KI0

- Veteran healing testimony from combat
  trauma and child abuse: https://youtu.be/
  diTqB88lKak

PTSD healing of veterans testimonies:

- https://youtu.be/uzoaqgYSXGg
- https://youtu.be/DCv8uM2WVx0
- https://youtu.be/RXM69gASPbw
- https://youtu.be/ihoeMuTWuZE
- https://youtu.be/1fkF7IYUrQ4

God Heals PTSD
Foundation

The God Heals PTSD Foundation provides education, training, resources, and awareness events that equip and educate to give treatment and restoration to those who have experienced trauma that continues to impact their present lives. The foundation provides resources including print, audio and video media, and social media platforms to raise awareness of the pervasiveness of the impact the memories and experiences of trauma have in culture.

The foundation also provides resources to chaplains, treatment centers, retreat centers for military veterans and active duty soldiers, and organizations dedicated to supporting military and first responders. The core message of the foundation is that God has provided healing and restoration to all forms of traumatic injury, and that healing can be experienced now.

FOR MORE INFORMATION

God Heals PTSD Foundation

131 Stonebridge Dr

Dillsburg, PA 17019

Email: godhealsptsd@gmail.com

Facebook: God Heals PTSD

Website: https://www.godhealsptsd.com/about-us

DR. MIKE HUTCHINGS
Executive Director, Mentor

About Dr. Michael Hutchings

Dr. Michael Hutchings has been in ministry to the church as senior pastor, church planter, counselor, and education director for 40 years. He has earned two doctoral degrees in ministry. His book *Coming Home: God Heals PTSD* shares the testimonies of healed cases of post-traumatic stress disorder (military and civilian) that he has personally witnessed through the power of healing prayer. He conducts "Healing PTSD" training seminars throughout the United States and four other countries, in churches, ministry centers, and military bases. He trains prayer ministers, clergy, chaplains, and counselors to utilize a healing prayer model to bring restoration to those suffering with PTSD.

He has worked as a licensed behavioral therapist in private practice counseling and was clinical coordinator for a counseling program serving homeless, runaway youth and their families.

He is currently the Director of Education for Global Awakening, an evangelistic ministry in Mechanicsburg, Pennsylvania. He directs Dr. Randy Clark's Global School of Supernatural Ministry and the Global Certification Programs. He is passionate about connecting pastors and leaders throughout the body of Christ to come together for transformation in their cities, and he strives to equip others to minister healing and wholeness to the world. He travels to churches and conferences near military bases in the United States, equipping churches to minister healing to those who suffer from PTSD. He has been married to his wife, Roxanne, for 35 years and has three children and five grandchildren.